Current
CONTROVERSIES

Rap Music and Culture

Other Books in the Current Controversies Series

CONTROVERSIES

Rap Music and Culture

Kate Burns, Book Editor

GREENHAVEN PRESS
A part of Gale, Cengage Learning

Detroit • New York • San Francisco • New Haven, Conn • Waterville, Maine • London

Christine Nasso, *Publisher*
Elizabeth Des Chenes, *Managing Editor*

© 2008 Greenhaven Press, a part of Gale, Cengage Learning

Gale and Greenhaven Press are registered trademarks used herein under license.

For more information, contact:
Greenhaven Press
27500 Drake Rd.
Farmington Hills, MI 48331-3535
Or you can visit our Internet site at gale.cengage.com

For product information and technology assistance, contact us at

Gale Customer Support, 1-800-877-4253
For permission to use material from this text or product, submit all requests online at www.cengage.com/permissions

Further permissions questions can be emailed to permissionrequest@cengage.com

Articles in Greenhaven Press anthologies are often edited for length to meet page requirements. In addition, original titles of these works are changed to clearly present the main thesis and to explicitly indicate the author's opinion. Every effort is made to ensure that Greenhaven Press accurately reflects the original intent of the authors. Every effort has been made to trace the owners of copyrighted material.

Cover image © PhotoAlto/SuperStock.

LIBRARY OF CONGRESS CATALOGING-IN-PUBLICATION DATA

Rap music and culture / Kate Burns, book editor.
    p. cm. -- (Current controversies)
Includes bibliographical references and index.
ISBN-13: 978-0-7377-3964-0 (hardcover)
ISBN-13: 978-0-7377-3965-7 (pbk.)
    1. Rap (Music)--Social aspects--Juvenile literature. 2. Hip-hop--Juvenile literature.
I. Burns, Kate, 1963-
    ML3918.R37R38 2008
    306.4'84249--dc22
                                                    2008017919

Printed in the United States of America
1 2 3 4 5 6 7 12 11 10 09 08

Contents

Chapter 1: Is Rap Culture a Significant American Cultural Movement?

Todd Boyd

Rap is an African American expressive tradition that has enabled minority youth to critique mainstream American culture and develop a unique hip-hop version of the American Dream. The limited vision of the civil rights era has given way to this new social movement that empowers young African Americans and Latinos to overcome obstacles in American life.

Yes: Rap Culture Is a Significant American Cultural Movement

Janice Rahn

Hip-hop graffiti is part of a larger hip-hop movement that includes hip-hop dancing, DJ-ing and MC-ing, and rap music. Like any other art form, hip-hop graffiti culture is structured with its own language, worldview, code of ethics, and artist hierarchy.

Carla Stalling Huntington

Hip-hop dance is an African American art form that has been adopted by mainstream American consumer culture. The commercialization of hip-hop music and dance threatens to reduce its recognition as an important art form.

Yes: Rap Culture Provides a Positive Outlet for Young People

No: Rap Culture Is Not a Constructive Medium for Young People

Chapter 3: Is Rap Music Harmful to Women?

Chapter 4: Does Rap Culture Perpetuate Violence?

Foreword

By definition, controversies are "discussions of questions in which opposing opinions clash" (*Webster's Twentieth Century Dictionary Unabridged*). Few would deny that controversies are a pervasive part of the human condition and exist on virtually every level of human enterprise. Controversies transpire between individuals and among groups, within nations and between nations. Controversies supply the grist necessary for progress by providing challenges and challengers to the status quo. They also create atmospheres where strife and warfare can flourish. A world without controversies would be a peaceful world; but it also would be, by and large, static and prosaic.

The Series' Purpose

The purpose of the *Current Controversies* series is to explore many of the social, political, and economic controversies dominating the national and international scenes today. Titles selected for inclusion in the series are highly focused and specific. For example, from the larger category of criminal justice, *Current Controversies* deals with specific topics such as police brutality, gun control, white collar crime, and others. The debates in *Current Controversies* also are presented in a useful, timeless fashion. Articles and book excerpts included in each title are selected if they contribute valuable, long-range ideas to the overall debate. And wherever possible, current information is enhanced with historical documents and other relevant materials. Thus, while individual titles are current in focus, every effort is made to ensure that they will not become quickly outdated. Books in the *Current Controversies* series will remain important resources for librarians, teachers, and students for many years.

In addition to keeping the titles focused and specific, great care is taken in the editorial format of each book in the series. Book introductions and chapter prefaces are offered to provide background material for readers. Chapters are organized around several key questions that are answered with diverse opinions representing all points on the political spectrum. Materials in each chapter include opinions in which authors clearly disagree as well as alternative opinions in which authors may agree on a broader issue but disagree on the possible solutions. In this way, the content of each volume in *Current Controversies* mirrors the mosaic of opinions encountered in society. Readers will quickly realize that there are many viable answers to these complex issues. By questioning each author's conclusions, students and casual readers can begin to develop the critical thinking skills so important to evaluating opinionated material.

Current Controversies is also ideal for controlled research. Each anthology in the series is composed of primary sources taken from a wide gamut of informational categories including periodicals, newspapers, books, U.S. and foreign government documents, and the publications of private and public organizations. Readers will find factual support for reports, debates, and research papers covering all areas of important issues. In addition, an annotated table of contents, an index, a book and periodical bibliography, and a list of organizations to contact are included in each book to expedite further research.

Perhaps more than ever before in history, people are confronted with diverse and contradictory information. During the Persian Gulf War, for example, the public was not only treated to minute-to-minute coverage of the war, it was also inundated with critiques of the coverage and countless analyses of the factors motivating U.S. involvement. Being able to sort through the plethora of opinions accompanying today's major issues, and to draw one's own conclusions, can be a complicated and frustrating struggle. It is the editors' hope that *Current Controversies* will help readers with this struggle.

Introduction

Exploring the topic of rap music and culture often gives rise to a question about terminology. Even quick reviews of the viewpoints that follow reveal that some authors refer to "rap music" and "rap culture" while others instead use the term "hip-hop." In contrast, a few authors interchange the two terms throughout a viewpoint. Is there a difference between "rap" and "hip-hop" or do the words mean the same thing? There are numerous answers to this question and the debate is controversial. Some use the two terms as if they are identical. A significant number of artists and fans assert that comparing the two is like comparing apples and oranges; "rap," to them, is one element in the larger cultural movement of "hip-hop." Others believe the difference between "rap" and "hip-hop" is a matter of quality.

The mainstream media most often use the two terms as if they are synonymous. Television and newspaper stories about fans, musicians, and the industry rarely distinguish between rap and hip-hop. Furthermore, the mainstream media's depiction of the culture is strikingly negative. In the article "The Hip-Hop Hype: Black Males Battle Stereotypes," music manager Blue Williams attributes negative media stereotypes to racial bigotry. He writes, "The problem is that American culture has such an inbred sense of racism, we don't even realize that anything that shows black men speaking in high voices and being aggressive is going to be perceived badly." Art Jones and Kim Deterline agree with Williams in "Fear of a Rap Planet:"

> Media stereotypes of black men as more violence-prone, and media's disproportionate focus on black crime (which is confused with the personas that rappers adopt), contribute to biased treatment of rap. The double standard applied to

rap music makes it easier to sell the idea that "gangsta rap" is "more" misogynist, racist, violent and just plain dangerous than other music.

Musicians and fans criticize the mainstream media's lack of knowledge about the complex world of rap music and hip-hop culture. One common oversight they particularly dislike is when terms are used without understanding what they mean within the culture. As Jeff Chang writes in his article "Hip-Hop is Not the Problem," most journalists "confuse commercial rap . . . with how hip-hop is lived" and therefore "miss the good that hip-hop does." Many agree with Chang that the tendency to disparage the whole culture is related to the same ignorance that also uncritically equates rap with hip-hop.

A famous quote by musician KRS-One represents a common perception within the culture about the difference between rap and hip-hop. "Hip-hop is something you live," he said, and "rap is something you do." Nationally renowned hip-hop historian Davey D. agrees, explaining that "One is part of a whole. Rap is part of a larger entity we call hip-hop, which is culture." Like many others, KRS-One and Davey D. relate "rap" to the tradition of MC-ing (or emceeing). In the early 1970s, the term "MC" was shorthand for "master of ceremonies," "microphone controller" or "music commentator." It defined a vocal style in which performers spoke rhythmically and in rhyme to a strong beat, introducing the DJs with which they worked and encouraging the crowd to dance and enjoy the music. As time went on, more people began using the term "rapper" interchangeably with "MC." Originally, the hip-hop movement was characterized by four elements: rapping, DJ-ing, breakdancing, and graffiti art. In this context, "rap" is one part of the larger culture of hip-hop.

Most agree this was certainly true in the early stages of the hip-hop movement, but some would argue that the two terms have evolved to indicate two different types of music. For the artists and fans who want to preserve the aesthetic and values of the early hip-hop movement, "rap" has become the word to stand for music that lacks integrity and promotes selfish individualism, materialism, and gratuitous violence. In contrast to the commercially successful rap musicians, those who prefer to call themselves hip-hop artists praise music that refuses to be silent about social and economic problems like racism, inner-city poverty and despair, and the need for collective action to improve the lives of poor minorities in America. Moreover, hip-hop musicians, in this sense, prioritize making artistically challenging, innovative music as opposed to music that makes money in the industry. Expressing this opinion of rap versus hip-hop, reporter Wendell T. Harrison of the University of Louisiana newspaper the *Reveille* writes, "It is hard to distinguish the two genres because the dividing line is as fine as the difference between fine art and stick figures. Hip-hop, like a classical art piece, does incite emotions. Stick figures and rap can only illustrate." He continues:

> It does not take someone with talent to rap. . . . In general, material gain is what most modern rappers seem to be about.

> When Nelly links his success to making money as opposed to the consciousness of his listeners, he is basically saying that he is not interested in the artistic aspect of his music or its power to inspire, but its ability to make him richer.

> Commercialism is the biggest enemy of the original hip-hop movement and ideally what separates rappers from hip-hop musicians.

This method of distinguishing rap from hip-hop is not accepted by all. Critics argue that it stereotypes commercially successful music and creates a caste system within the music culture. Such a sharp dichotomy between good and bad music, they argue, fails to account for the infinite variety of rap and hip-hop music, some of it "underground" and some of it achieving mass popularity. *Current Controversies: Rap Music and Culture* delivers a thought-provoking assortment of research and commentary about rap music and hip-hop culture. Selections address the significance of the movement in American culture, speculate about its relationship to youth culture, and examine the controversies of sexism and violence in rap music.

CHAPTER 1

Is Rap Culture a Significant American Cultural Movement?

Overview: Rap Culture Is an American Social Movement

Todd Boyd

Todd Boyd is a professor in critical studies at the University of Southern California School of Cinema-Television. His books include Am I Black Enough for You? Popular Culture from the 'Hood and Beyond *and* The New H.N.I.C.: The Death of Civil Rights and the Reign of Hip-Hop.

> I don't want much/f--- I drove every car/some nice cooked food/some nice clean draws/bird ass n---as I don't mean to ruffle y'all/I know you're waitin' in wings/but I'm doin' my thing. —Jay-Z, "Heart of the City"

> Words are more powerful than fists. —Muhammad Ali, on *The Mike Douglas Show*, July 17, 1974.

I can remember vividly the first time I heard "Rapper's Delight" by the Sugarhill Gang. A couple of my boys had come by to scoop me up and when I got in that 1977 Ford Granada that day, all they could talk about was this new song they had heard on the radio. The problem was they couldn't really describe the tune. They didn't know the name of the song, nor did they know who it was by. They just kept saying that it was different, that it was like *talkin' over some beats*. They had heard it a few times on the radio, and assured me that it would come on again. As a matter of fact, we rode around that day until it eventually came on the radio.

I can hear it now, "What you hear is not a test/I'm rappin' to the beat...." As the song moved through each verse, from Wonder Mike, Big Bank Hank, and Master Gee, the momentum built to an incredible crescendo. Remember, this is 1979,

19

back in the day, before all the radio stations were these corporate conglomerates with no unique identity that played the same shit repeatedly in a predictable fashion. No, this was when they played the extended version of "Rapper's Delight," all seven or eight minutes of it. I really liked the last verse on that extended version, "[H]ave you ever gone over to a friend's house to eat/and the food just ain't no good?/I mean the macaroni's soggy/the beans all mushed/and the chicken taste like wood." That was the shit!

"Rapper's Delight" was like a bolt of lightning for me. Everyone else I knew had been listening to Michael Jackson's *Off the Wall* album as if it were the last record they would ever hear. Now, that record was cool, and it now seems even better, considering that it was the last album Michael made before completely losing his mind, but considering that so many other people were into it, I needed to have something else to listen to, something else to distinguish my musical taste from the masses. "Rapper's Delight" would serve that purpose and it would open a door into a culture and a worldview that would still continue to inform me, even today.

I couldn't help myself. I listened to this over and over again. It was so transgressive, so vulgar, and I loved it.

I was committed to learning every word in every verse of that song. We even had a contest to see who could recite the whole song from memory. I won that contest going away. It got to the point where cats would come to me in the lunchroom and ask me to rap it for them, and I gladly obliged. A short time thereafter I heard Kurtis Blow do "Christmas Rappin" and it was on, again. I loved this new rap thing, better than a hog loved slop!

The Rhythm of Language

Language has always been fascinating to me. This is why rap appealed to me so much. It was a new language. It drew on the style that I had heard growing up, all around me. From the preacher's rap to the disc jockey's rap on the radio, to the n---as on the corner who would use these clever rhymes as a way of identifying themselves. I remember once when I was real young and I got a new tape recorder for Christmas that year, and I was going around taping whatever I could. This n---a down the street, Eddie Bullock, asked me to let him say something on the recorder. I hesitated, and told him not to say no shit that would get me in trouble with Mom Dukes, and he agreed not to. Of course, when he got the mic in his hand, he went off, signifying and "playing the dozens."

Though I wanted to stop him, some magnetic force held me back. I was momentarily frozen in my steps. He was mesmerizing. Though I knew I had to erase this before Mom Dukes heard it, and I was pissed that he had done just what I asked him not to do, I couldn't help myself. I listened to this over and over again. It was so transgressive, so vulgar, and I loved it.

I was impressed by both the rhyming style and the fact that Eddie seemed to be waiting for the opportunity to say this. He had a huge grin on his face when he let out his words. See, Eddie was one of these cats, like a lot of other Brothas, who the school system had decided was "retarded" and he was isolated in this segregated world known as "Special Ed," so he didn't really socialize with the rest of us too much, though we all knew him. Well, on that day, Eddie might have been deemed "retarded" by the mainstream White establishment, here represented by the school system, but to me, he was a wordsmith of the highest order.

Word Power

The power of the word has always impressed me, especially, I must admit, its transgressive qualities. Though as a child I was surrounded by many Black people, Black men in particular, who had no control of their lives in the outside world, who were truly unfulfilled in their quest for self empowerment, who had no agency whatsoever but who had absolute command of the words that came out of their mouths. It made no difference what kind of inferior posture they had to assume on a daily basis, what kind of shit they had to take from the "White man," they had complete control of their words, their conversation. Again, this ranged from the many "jackleg" preachers I had heard to the coldest pimps you ever wanted to meet. Language was their thing, no doubt.

A short time after I immersed myself in this evolving rap thing, I heard Gil Scot-Heron for the first time. Shortly after the election of [U.S. president] Ronald Reagan, I heard Scot-Heron's tune "B Movie," which was an engaged critique of the direction the country was moving after the election of such a right-wing figure as Reagan. Man, that song still rings in my head today. Though I was only sixteen and not yet legal to vote, Scot-Heron's words turned me into an impassioned Reagan-hater. Now, many people would not consider Gil Scot-Heron hip hop because of his age, but his ability to weave sly metaphor with political analysis, and still rhyme tight, was incredible, and very much formative relative to what would become hip hop. I was especially fond of the way he listed the warmongers who dotted Reagan's first cabinet: George "Papa Doc" Bush [George H.W. Bush], Casper "The Defensive" Weinberger [defense secretary], and "Atilla the Haig" [Secretary of State Alexander Haig]. Scot-Heron's point that Reagan's highest accomplishment in Hollywood [as an actor before becoming a politician] was playing second to the monkey Bonzo was not lost on me. I began to get deeper and deeper into politics at that time, studying the cabinet, scrutinizing Reagan's "voodoo economics," and counting the days until this clown would no longer be in office. Well, of course, I was counting for a long time.

> A child is born with no state of mind/blind to the ways of mankind/God is smilin' on you/but he's frownin' too/cause only God knows what you'll go through. —Grand Master Flash and the Furious Five, featuring Melle Mel, "The Message"

All of this came to a head during my first semester in college, in the summer of 1982 at the University of Florida. Some cats who hailed from the infamous "Bucktown" (Overtown) section of Miami and who lived downstairs from me in the dorm had taken their financial aid money and purchased a new stereo, and they had a gang of albums to boot. They kept playing this twelve-inch record by Grand Master Flash and the Furious Five, featuring Melle Mel. That shit was so dope! Of course, the record I'm referring to is "The Message," one of the most important songs ever made.

It is at once humorous and a weapon of guerilla warfare against the sophisticated technology of the dominant order.

"The Message" . . . combined the dopest rhymes with a most astute level of political commentary on the effect Reagan's policies were having on the Black community. I couldn't stop listening to "The Message." Again, everybody else was listening to Michael Jackson's *Thriller* album and watching his groundbreaking videos by now, and so I really needed another outlet. I had grown to hate Michael, who was trying to look more and more like a White person with every passing day. The fact that so many people across campus, Black, White, male, female, were listening to the same thing made me nervous.

Back Talk, Black Talk

Though I did not grow up in New York, I have been a fan of hip hop ever since it made its way out of the Five Boroughs [Manhattan, Bronx, Queens, Staten Island, and Brooklyn]. I have been listening ever since. What I find so compelling is the way in which this relatively simple form of communication, rhymes over beats, however you slice it, is truly quite complex. Because Black people have always had to make do with so little, the relative abundance of one's own words is at times all we have to use in fighting against a corrupt and vicious society.

This is why hip hop is so important, and why it speaks to so many. It is at once humorous *and* a weapon of guerilla warfare against the sophisticated technology of the dominant order. Hip hop speaks in a code that allows people to communicate with one another beyond the eavesdropping that those in power often engage in. Like a lyrical tower of Babel [structure described in the Bible that united humanity], hip hop's confounding influence has at times had an ominous effect on society. For those who identify themselves with the mainstream, be they Black, White, or otherwise, hip hop is a pariah, something you want to get rid of because it attempts to tell the truth, in spite of the consequences that might accompany the telling of this truth.

When [comedian] Chris Rock engages the hip hop practice of keepin' it real, he is tearing down the walls of secrecy that for too long have stifled the Black expressive tradition. It makes no difference who hears it, it needs to be said, and it needs to be said by someone who clearly has the best interests of his people at heart, however acerbic or caustic it might be otherwise. There is an attempt at honesty here that supersedes moral convention or racial protocol.

Revealing the Real

The very fact that hip hop continues to look for that which is real, in a world that can be so fake otherwise, is again a testament to hip hop's enduring significance. It is the desire to uncover the real, however elusive this quest might be, that makes hip hop such a worthwhile enterprise. While the debates in hip hop about who's real and who's not might be redundant on occasion, it reflects a larger interest in finding something substantive, deciphering some meaning in life that can far too often seem a waste of time.

It takes money to live in America, and it takes a lot of money if you want anything beyond the bare minimum. In spite of whatever struggles Black people have encountered in this society, the struggle to live a decent life is one that never subsides, no matter how much money you get.

When Danny Glover, a well-known [African American] actor made famous by the immense popularity of a franchise like the *Lethal Weapon* films, cannot get a cab in New York City, there is something seriously wrong. It's not that Glover is hard to recognize either. Do you realize how many people have seen those *Lethal Weapon* films? I bet [Glover's white costar] Mel Gibson never got passed up by a cab before!

What is even more ironic is that for all those cabdrivers who would pass up Danny Glover, those same people would, more than likely, still want his autograph. This is the dilemma of being Black in America. You're at once loved for your unique contribution to society and simultaneously hated for being who you are. This irreconcilable difference is the push and pull that makes life nearly impossible to navigate. As Jay-Z says, "Can I live?"

The Dream, American Style

In my mind, the pursuit of money, capital, cheese, paper, scrilla, fetti, and cake is a time-honored tradition in American culture. We have tended to praise those individuals who have pursued this capital, especially those who have done so with a particular flair. Figures like [businessman and politician] Joe Kennedy, of old, started out selling bootleg liquor and went on to enshrine his family as American royalty, his hustlin' past neatly erased from the picture. Or, look at America's continued fascination with mobsters, from Lucky Luciano to Meyer Lansky, from [fictional characters] Don Corleone to, most recently, Tony Soprano. In each case, there was and remains a fascination with these individuals, their flamboyant lifestyle, and their penchant for drama. If we pay attention to the most cent case here, the overwhelmingly popular HBO program, *The Sopranos*, we can see this trend anew.

The Sopranos features an intimate portrayal of your typical suburban New Jersey family; the father, Tony; the mother, Carmela; their daughter, Meadow, who is a student at Columbia University; and their at times wayward young son, Anthony Jr. There is also the representation of an extended family that includes Tony's now-deceased mother, his conniving sister, and his Uncle Jr. The representation of their world is not unlike most other images of the suburban family, with the exception that the head of the household, Tony, is a mob boss. Now, *The Sopranos* is a wonderful television offering, no doubt. Its refreshing take on the suburban ideal is quite enjoyable and often enlightening as a form of popular culture.

A Black Version of *The Sopranos*

Yet, can we imagine a similar program on, say, a Black drug kingpin? A program where the Black criminal figure is afforded a family and shown to practice his craft, while being able to skirt the law and remain viable, so as to further our investigation into the ironic nuances of daily family life? Not only is this something we cannot imagine, we know it would never exist. Even if by some strange stretch of the imagination it did, the connotations would still be drastically different.

Hip hop is about the real, not the literal.

No one, Black, White, or otherwise, is interested in the motivation of a Black drug dealer. No one wants to sympathize with a figure like this. No one assumes that a person like this deserves anything other than the penitentiary or death. This is an unevolved figure who is dehumanized from the jump. It is a figure that deserves no consideration whatsoever beyond consideration of shackles on his feet or a bullet in his . . . head!

Well, there are elements of hip hop that function very much like the Black version of *The Sopranos*. In this case, the intricate nuances of the life of a Black gangsta, through the voice of hip hop, gets the same sort of treatment and regard as that of the fictional Tony Soprano. If the culture can fictionalize the life of a White mobster, be it a truly fictional one like Tony, or a real-life figure like John Gotti, why can't the same be accorded a hip hop artist who uses the medium to articulate his or her life in streets? Why is it that when a Black artist filters and interprets his or her culture through a fictional medium, it is assumed to be literal. Again, hip hop is about the real, not the literal. It is about using a stylistic mode of address known as realism to render the speakers' lives for their listeners.

Hip hop artists are charged with articulating what they see, and the best of them do it with the same precision, the same distinct approach, as any great writer of fiction would. Hip hop is an art form, and like any art form, it, of course, is rooted in some sense of reality, for it must draw its impetus from somewhere. Yet so many want to read it literally, as though a rapper is actually cocking the trigger of a gun, while spittin' sixteen bars in the studio. . . .

The Civil Rights Era

At the end of the day we live in a society where culture assumes a very prominent role. It was such in the 1960s that the civil rights movement became a culture of sorts, a culture with its own music, its own images, its own way of being. This culture was in subsequent years repackaged and injected into our collective memory via imagery. I often point to the groundbreaking Blackside documentary series *Eyes on the Prize* which was originally broadcast on PBS during the late 1980s as a perfect example of how the era of the civil rights movement will be remembered. PBS has come to assume a prominent place in the retelling of various aspects of the

American historical narrative, and this being the case, *Eyes on the Prize* serves as the representation of record, if you will, when it comes to visualizing civil rights. In addition, Hollywood has now consistently produced films that are set during the civil rights era and almost suggest that racism and its attendant difficulties are a thing of the past, safe to be relegated to a history far removed from contemporary culture. It is as though racism is historical and not contemporary.

The fact that the events of the civil rights era lend themselves so well to being represented visually has made it so that society as a whole uses these visual images—what I like to refer to as "dogs and waterhoses"—to forever define how race and racism function. Yet, in the aftermath of this perfectly visual time, contemporary race and its subtle and nuanced functions often get dismissed, for it is now routinely assumed that in order for racism to exist it must live up to these lofty standards set by the spectacular visual images of the past.

The other lingering remnant of civil rights lies in the way that we now assume that this era defined Blackness for the ages, that in order to be truly Black, one had to have been attacked by dogs and doused with waterhoses, that one had to be forced to get up from a segregated lunch counter in order to claim to be truly Black. In all of this, Blackness was cloaked in suffering, and defined by the degree to which one had been abused.

A Limited Vision

My point is not to make light of this but, instead, to point out the limited nature of continually pursuing such a dead-end street. If Blackness can be defended only as suffering, then what was the point of pursuing a free and open society? What was the point of trying to knock down the walls that denied Black people the opportunity for advancement when all we were going to do was erect new walls that contained our progress, and made that progress hostage to the struggles that attempted to make advancement possible in the first place?

America has now turned Martin Luther King Jr.'s dream into a long weekend. In other words, civil rights has passed; get over it!

The civil rights movement was dour, it was serious, and it was ultimately heavy in the way that it bore on the soul. Many people, Black, White, and otherwise, have embraced this era while rejecting any subsequent era as failing to live up to the standards of the one previous. It is within their best interest to hold civil rights up as the "be-all-end-all" of race in America. This is not only self-serving, it is utterly regressive.

America has now turned Martin Luther King Jr.'s dream into a long weekend. In other words, civil rights has passed; get over it!

The Hip Hop Generation

Hip hop has not completely forgotten civil rights though. No, as a matter of fact, hip hop has done a great deal to firmly place the moments of this era in a larger historical context. The music and culture have always attempted to remember the past, yet have also urged us to move forward.

What hip hop has done is taught us that true freedom and liberation can begin only if we move beyond being concerned about doing things the "right" way. Hip hop continually embraces contradiction as opposed to trying to make everything seem perfect, trying to make everything conform to a dominant moral idea.

At this point, one cannot even begin to discuss American culture without dealing with Black culture, and this continues to increase with each passing day. Recognizing this cultural impact, hip hop then, in my mind, is ultimately the model that best allows us to understand the present generation of

African Americans, and by extension, the present generation of Americans. This culture allows us to understand how the present generation is so very different from previous generations of Black people, for the present generation has grown up at a different time in history.

Hip hop also allows us to begin to understand how this generation might make sense of their future, which will most certainly be different from the way that previous generations have reconciled their issues. In addition, hip hop is a prominent vehicle for expression, for culture has been one of the more visible areas of society where Blacks have consistently had the most representation.

The Times Are Changing

My words are not intended as a diss of civil rights. No. It is amazingly obvious what a profound effect that moment in history has had on the world, and it certainly hit home in America. Civil rights will forever be an integral part of the American master narrative.

Yes, it is unfortunate that many people's lives were lost fighting in this struggle. Yes, it is quite unfortunate also that people had to fight for this in the first place. Blood was shed, no doubt. It is also not as though I'm saying that racism has disappeared today either. By no means has it disappeared. I am not even saying that it has subsided, though it has, like the times themselves, been altered to fit a new age.

What I am saying is that we cannot live in the past forever. Civil rights had its day; now it is time to move out of the way. Civil rights was a struggle, and it remains an ongoing struggle for all disenfranchised people of color to pursue their civil rights. But many in the civil rights era have for too long gloated in a sanctimonious fashion, assuming that their day would never come to an end. This arrogant posture did little to inspire a new generation but went a long way toward alienating them. The posture of civil rights was such that it made future generations uncomfortable having to wear such restraints as they attempted to represent themselves.

Hip hop is a lifestyle. It is an ideology. It is a mode of being. It is an all-encompassing life force.

Hip hop has allowed them to throw off those shackles, and though it is far from perfect, it does attempt to navigate the world in a very different way. Having survived the naysayers who from the beginning said that hip hop was only a musical trend, the culture, some twenty-plus years later, represents something far beyond music even.

Hip Hop Is a Solid Movement

Hip hop is a lifestyle. It is an ideology, it is a mode of being. It is an all-encompassing life force that far supersedes any dismissive tactic from those whom Flava Flav once chided as "nonbelievers." No matter how much you want to dismiss it, it is still here, having passed many tests, and poised to triumph even more in the future.

Hip hop is a testament to overcoming the obstacles that American life often imposes on its Black and Latino subjects, and in this, it is a model of what "we shall overcome" means in the modern world. To quote someone who, were he alive today, would most certainly find his voice in hip hop, William Shakespeare: hip hop, maybe more than any other contemporary form, truly embodies "the sweet uses of adversity/which, like the toad ugly and venomous/wears yet a precious/jewel in his head."

Hip-Hop Graffiti Is a Significant American Art Form

Janice Rahn

Janice Rahn is a professor of art education at the University of Lethbridge, Canada, and the author of Painting Without Permission: Hip-Hop Graffiti Subculture.

Although graffiti was being scrawled in black letters, symbols, and images on subway trains and public property in the 1960s, it wasn't until a decade later that graffiti emerged as part of a hip-hop movement in combination with breakdancing, DJ-ing, and MC-ing. By the late '80s all these forms were being performed simultaneously as an expression of hip-hop culture. . . .

Tricia Rose in *Black Noise* chronicles the urban context of the Bronx [New York] during the 1970s. The South Bronx especially, became notorious for gangs, burnt-out abandoned buildings, drugs, and poverty. This came about through a combination of postindustrial conditions exacerbated by the community relocation and destruction largely initiated and executed by Robert Moses in the implementation of the Cross Bronx Expressway. [Rose writes,] "like many of his public works projects, Moses' Cross Bronx Expressway supported the interest of the upper classes against the interest of the poor and intensified the development of the vast economic and social inequalities that characterize contemporary New York."

Hip-hop culture emerged from these ashes of destruction to give youth hope and a sense of identity formed through peer support and competition between individuals and groups. Abandoned by the social service cuts and the support of larger institutional structures due to the bankruptcy of New York in the 1970s, creative youth made do with discarded technology and drove each other to achieve through the never-ending battles of hip-hop's competitive street entertainment. [Critic Robert Verain writes,] "Competition, of course is the very essence of every aspect of hip-hop culture, be it graffiti, MC-ing, DJ-ing—'what makes it real is the battle,' says Kid Freeze."

Today there is still an East Coast/West Coast rivalry, primarily between Los Angeles and New York, that is highlighted in the rap lyrics and some messages on freight-train graffiti. Regional differences and rivalries still exist, despite the fact that hip-hop graffiti has become a global community via the Web and subculture magazines.

Writers like to distinguish themselves from taggers. One becomes a writer when he or she has developed an individual style within the tradition of hip-hop.

Hip-Hop Graffiti

Early graffiti writers who grew out of the hip-hop culture are harder to trace due to the lack of a written history and the short life span of the medium. Graffiti tends to be cleaned off or *buffed* by the authorities or painted over by rival artists. Many sources cited TAKI 183 in New York as the originator of the *tag*. Renaming oneself is an important part of the culture. . . . The tag is a writer's name that is drawn like a calligraphic symbol, usually with a marker or spray paint. If he/she writes with a marker on a street sign, it is a tag; if the name is painted large with style and multicolors, it is called a "piece," though it is still a tag name. In 1971 the *New York Times* ran a story on TAKI 183, a Greek teenager named Demetrius who wrote his name everywhere while working as a messenger, traveling by subway across the city. The article prompted a wave of copycats who also adopted a name/number pseudonym (EVA 62, ELSIE 137). Eventually each tagger developed his or her own individual formal style to express identity and status among peers.

Bombing the commuter trains became too hard and unrealistic when the New York City transit system began to immediately pull trains from the line to be buffed (chemically washed). Gradually, large-scale works and, later, any graffiti became rare on subway trains and the more accessible freight trains (Fr8s) became the target of choice for contemporary graf artists. The emphasis shifted from quantity to quality and high visibility of the tag. *Fr8s* is a vernacular spelling of "freights" as in freight trains. Freights are increasing in popularity because they travel across the continent, like a traveling exhibition to be viewed by other writers. The practice of writing on freights, the emergence of graffiti fanzines [fan magazines], and the Internet spread trends quickly and allowed for efficient communication among writers in both urban and rural centers across North America. Evidence of this was seen in the high-quality, large-scale graffiti found in small towns throughout Canada and the United States and in black books being kept in Cree [Native American] communities in northern Quebec.

Taggers Versus Writers

In New York City in the 1980s, tags became like an uninterrupted citywide wallpaper pattern on moving vans, streetlights, bus windows, and buildings. As tags competed for space, they also competed for skills and style. The tag is considered the crudest and most prevalent form of graffiti. Most writers begin as taggers and graduate to larger pieces as they grow bolder and acquire technical skills. The practice began as "tag" in a game sense in New York City, where someone would hit a blank wall and others would follow, respect going to those who covered the most ground. Taggers who go on to develop elaborate painting styles identity themselves as *writers.*

Taggers who never produce large pieces are called *Scribblers* and *Toys* and have little status. In the mid-1980s, graffiti writers set standards and mutually acknowledged a level of skills that had to be reached to merit the title of *writer* rather than the inferior *toy*. A toy is a person who attempts graf without skills or the commitment to learn from other writers. A toy has not paid his dues and is not respected. A toy's work is *wack*: lacking in skill and obviously inferior. Writers like to distinguish themselves from taggers. One becomes a writer when he or she has developed an individual style within the tradition of hip-hop. The writer has developed painting skills to a level where the community accepts his or her presence and work. A *crew* is a loose association of graf writers. A single artist or a crew can do large pieces. One writer may belong to any number of crews. Crews either paint together or acknowledge each other by citing the names of their crew or mentors around the edges of a graffiti piece. A crew is often mislabeled as a *gang*. A group forms a crew to paint, to "battle" (as breakdancers), or to compete for skills and style, not for violence. Crews will photograph each other's work, share drawings, compete with other crews, and plan painting trips to favored locations. Writers may steal paint if they lack the funds but other illegal activities are avoided. Most sources claimed that graffiti provided a nonviolent alternative to gangs where young people could satisfy the same need to belong and identify with the lifestyle of a group.

Influences spread quickly through fanzines, on freight trains crossing the country and especially via Web sites.

A *fanzine* is a magazine devoted to a specific phenomenon. Some examples are *12 oz. Prophet* (hip-hop graffiti), *RIG* (for and by window washers), or *MotorBooty* (Detroit music and news). Fanzines are about individual obsessions which are self-published, photocopied, stapled, and distributed by and for fans within the context of other fanzine writers. Fanzines are written not for profit but sometimes they gain popularity within the fanzine network and become glossy magazines. One example, *Giant Robot*, began as a homemade fanzine but is now a professionally printed quarterly about Asian culture in North America. Graffiti fanzines exist within the network of the fanzine culture that has helped to make graffiti more mainstream.

Influences of Graffiti Pioneers

A great deal of reference and reverence is given to graffiti "elders" who invented styles and were the first to practice tagging and piecing in a substantial way. Names that come up often are FUTURA 2000, BLADE, ZEPHYR, PHASE 2 (who came up with a bubble-letter style), LADY PINK (one of the few women mentioned), and TAKI 183. These writers set standards and styles that continue to be used and expanded upon today. Beyond these first few names, any attempt to cite a concise genealogy of graffiti quickly becomes convoluted. Writers would change their names, adopt multiple names, and belong to any number of crews.

As styles were adopted and mastered they spread from city to city, ever evolving, and cross-fertilizing innovations of individual writers. For example, a current trend in graf is to simulate a three-dimensional effect. No one graf artist is associated with having developed this method. In its infancy in the late 1970s, graf spread and changed slowly, via artists traveling to or from urban centers to pick up these skills. As the movement caught on, these images appeared in movies and rap music videos. Now influences spread quickly through fanzines, on freight trains crossing the country and especially via Web sites.

From Margin to Mainstream

Mainstream interpretations of hip-hop culture acknowledged the multiple roles that evolved in relation to each other. For example, *Beat Street* a Hollywood-produced hip-hop film by Harry Belafonte in 1984, focused on breakdancing but included graffiti and hip-hop music. The lead character was a graf artist as well as a dancer. The movie was set in the Bronx in the hangouts of artists, but it lacked authenticity since actors were hired to portray roles much younger than themselves and to imitate street talk. It became characteristic of hip-hop movies and rap videos to be situated in inner-city neighborhoods. Identity in hip-hop is tied in with specific locations. *Wild Style*, a 1981 film by indie filmmaker Charlie Ahearn, was the first feature-length film about hip-hop culture. It portrayed real-life graffiti writers and b-boys [followers of hip-hop culture] who acted out their authentic roles in relation to the SoHo art scene.

Graffiti's influence on mainstream modern art goes back to Jean Dubuffet and Pablo Picasso, who were attracted to "graffiti" from other cultures and "outsider" art. Ancient forms of graffiti influenced abstract expressionists such as Jackson Pollock and Cy Twombly, and by the 1980s graffiti had become completely co-opted by the mainstream art world through artists such as Keith Haring and Jean-Michel Basquiat. For a brief time in the 1980s, the downtown art galleries looked inquisitively at graffiti culture as "natural" exotics. Artists like Basquiat and Haring played up to this image of being wildly primitive. Both these artists died tragically and have become mythologized in movies and blockbuster museum exhibits. Keith Haring images help to sell t-shirts, coffee cups, calendars, and other products in the museum store.

Hip-hop graffiti culture has established an ethical code that resists the move away from their street-culture roots.

Recently, in urban centers such as Montreal and Toronto [Canada], specialty stores have opened that exclusively cater to a hip-hop clientele with clothing, graffiti equipment, and fanzines. Spray nozzles (caps), which in the past were stolen from other aerosol products for their different spray patterns, are now mass-produced and sold. Ad agencies such as Murad (Toronto and Montreal) now hire graffiti writers to paint large outdoor murals advertising jeans, beer, and movies. The World Wide Web includes an ever-increasing number of graffiti sites that link cities, names, and images like a gallery and reference manual. This gives the appearance of an emerging organizational structure for the culture. Graffiti conventions are being announced and writers are easily located, facilitating a network.

Hip-hop graffiti culture has established an ethical code that resists the move away from their street-culture roots into the realms of popular culture, commercialization, and the Internet. This code is known as "keeping it real" and, generally, any writer who appears to have "sold out" is snubbed. There seems to be a great deal of posturing within the community concerning the preservation of hip-hop ideals. For example, if a writer does not perform illegally, he/she may be criticized for not "keeping it real." Some writers point out that Web sites and fanzines made the culture too easy to discover. They want to maintain hip-hop as a street culture where beginners have to learn about tools, techniques, and styles in the streets. However, other writers consider anything that extends appreciation of their art around the world to be great. . . .

Skills and Respect

Most writers talk about skills and techniques as a fundamental basis of hip-hop graffiti. A writer who attempts a large piece without the necessary skills will be criticized for polluting the environment and giving hip-hop a bad reputation. The large piece is the measurement for earning respect for writers. Respect is a word that often comes up. Respect is attained and maintained by honing skills and keeping a high profile by continually "getting it up." *Dis* is short for "disrespect." A writer "disses" by criticizing or *crossing out* (paint over or disfigure) a piece. If this happens enough times, the writer being dissed will most likely quit. Therefore writers practice in their black books before they consider attempting a large piece.

A writer can lose respect and be "dissed" for a variety of infractions: selling work or avoiding illegal painting in favor of legal walls, continually crossing out other writers' work with no cause, overtly seeking media attention, and informing on fellow writers to the police. Another way to lose favor includes *biting*. A writer who copies another's style is "biting" that style. Respect is given to previous generations of writers for paying their dues. However, respect can be lost if older writers are perceived to be "selling out" by commercializing their work or opening a store.

The goal is to be famous within the hip-hop culture and not necessarily outside it.

The attitude to fame among writers in the graffiti community is paradoxical. Writers desire the notoriety of having their name painted everywhere and wish to receive the recognition for it, but they cannot appear to want this recognition too badly. A writer must be discreet about any media attention, despite the amount, to retain his or her standing. Individuals who are perceived to be obsessed with being interviewed and photographed, or claim to speak for the graf community at large, will eventually be dissed and crossed out.

Writers who are seen as focused and committed to piecing and acquiring skills while downplaying their fame are held in the highest esteem. The goal is to be famous within the hip-hop culture and not necessarily outside it. This is part of *keeping it real*. This ambiguous phrase has multiple meanings. . . . Old school writers interpret it to mean that hip-hop graffiti should maintain the traditions that were developed in its origins as a street culture. However, for some hip-hop adherents, "keeping it real" is a restrictive ethic that reinforces the status quo and disregards innovation.

Graffiti Language

It has been necessary to continually define terms throughout this ... [viewpoint] since graffiti writers treat language in the same manner that graf writers adapt the alphabet. English is distorted, adapted, and blurred with other languages until it begins to sound like a code or a new dialect that identifies a different school of thought. Two terms that are used extensively within hip-hop are *old school* and *new school*. *Old school* refers to the historical New York hip-hop tradition with no definitive date. SEAZ and FLOW are examples of old school writers in Montreal who model themselves after the traditional New York style. An old school graf style may refer to a lettering style from 1971 or 1987. Similar terms for this are *back in the day*, *old days*, and *old style*.

New school describes an innovative approach to hip-hop writing. Generally, this can mean any typical work from 1994 and onward, though this term always depends on the users' context.... I use the terms *old school* and *new school* to distinguish between two different groups of writers within Montreal. Another term for "new school" is *new style*.

Various terms are used exclusively to describe hip-hop graffiti. A *burner* is an exceptional piece. If writers beat a competitor with their work, they *burn* the competition. If the graf is highly regarded, it is *dope*, *fresh*, or *the shit* as in DAES's interview, "That throw-up is the shit! It's so amazing!"

Some positive hip-hop adjectives include *crazy* (meaning "really" as in "crazy big") and *mad* (quantity, as in "mad graf"). To *front* is to hassle or provoke a fight with a competitor. Graf artists can have a *battle* where each writer "fronts" the other with painting techniques, although fronting can also refer to violence. If writers paint or tag a surface, they *hit* it.

An area that is covered with a large quantity of tags or pieces has been *hit up*. If writers are extremely prolific, they *kill*.

Writers sometimes invent acronyms to include in their large pieces. FLOW's crew is called S.A.T. which stands for "Smashing All Toys." TIMER uses B.A.M. which means "Beyond All Misfortunes."

Old School

Anyone who is really into old school hip-hop adheres to the rules down to the way they tie their running shoes. I asked Robert Segovia, a devoted hip-hop breakdancer from 1981 to 1986, about the obsession of shoelaces. He e-mailed the following account of the most important things that he remembered about tying shoelaces.

> At that time neon colors were getting big. One had to match the laces in a color matching the shoe. Both high tops and low tops were popular at the time. Tying them was all about precision and obsession. We tried to tie them perfectly, with no extra lace hanging or tied anywhere. After you laced the pattern, you would cut the extra lace, re-tape or burn the ends and tuck them away somewhere on the shoe so you had a clean look. I remember three patterns of tying the laces:
>
> 1. The first pattern is classic military style in straight-across bands. The idea is to have perfect widths, even watching where the lace pokes out of the hole so the laces are even. As well, one watches that the laces overlap slightly—consistently.
>
> 2. The second pattern is a v-pattern. The first line at the toe is horizontal, and then all bands make a repeating v-pattern. . . . When you do the other shoe, you must remember to reflect or overlap the opposite side so that the two shoes, when placed beside one another, have symmetry. If the outer edge on the right shoe has top overlap, then the outer edge on the left shoe must also have top overlap. Symmetry is very important.

3. The third pattern I remember was the basket weave. This is done by starting the shoe as straight bands, but then taking a second lace and basket weaving a pattern into the shoe. So this style takes four laces, but one can pick complementary colors, etc. As well, the same rules apply: use symmetry, no loose laces hanging, perfect spacing, etc. Of course after breakin' (breakdancing) you had to fix them all over.

This obsession for order is one example of how traditional hip-hop culture is a community defined by codes of behavior, dress, and language. The paradox of the hip-hop community is this desire for conformity of language, dress, and rules of ethics when graffiti is known for its resistance against systems of authority.

Hip-Hop Dance Is a Significant American Art Form

Carla Stalling Huntington

Carla Stalling Huntington is a professor of marketing at Missouri Southern State University and the author of numerous articles and books on dance and the performing arts, including Hip Hop Dance: Meanings and Messages.

> "The association of words with dance has a long history that goes back to precolonial West African empires . . . dance can be understood as a form of orality." —Francesca Castaldi, *Choreographies of African Identities*

I know hip hop dance when I see it but it cannot be touched. It can be described, sold, and transmitted; learned, choreographed and commoditized. Used. Profited from.

However, hip hop dance writes, theories, interprets, and communicates.

The Appeal of Hip Hop Dance

This rich, wondrous text, once written but then not theorizing, interpreting or communicating, finds distribution through television commercials and programs, commercial films, music videos, instructional videos, at concerts, in commercial dance studios, at cheerleading and marching band locales, online, in graphic and cartoon form, and in private consumption spaces. These points of intake cater to a diverse set of people who come from many divisions of life.

One finds housewives wanting to learn, suburban youth identifying with its misinterpreted messages and meanings, Indians, Asians, Australians, Europeans, Africans, Euro American whites, African Americans and many in between who want to too. Learning not in the streets of inner city ghettos but in suburban studios whose products include 1) every-child-gets-a-feel-good-about-him-or-herself-medal won at a hip hop dance competition even if they cannot dance and; 2) recital numbers seen by proud yet uneasy parents where the youngsters shake behinds and stand like non-threatening original gangsters they saw on JC Penney commercials for back to school clothes.

Hip hop dance provides something for almost everyone.

And moreover, some of those who do not overtly engage in learning the dance are themselves often intrigued at the sheer athleticism of the text. I have witnessed middle-aged white women trying out the moves behind the closed doors of empty but adjacent dance studio spaces when they think no one is looking and their children are taking class. They laughed embarrassedly when they saw me looking at them trying to do The Runnin' Man. They said it was better than aerobics. I smiled and nodded with them in agreement.

Something for Everyone

Why the deep connect with hip hop dance? What strength does it bring? What understanding does it possess? Is it because it is inherently an African American cultural artifact that has succeeded in its export in becoming more American than African? Is it because it is cool and to be American is to be a cool cultural consumption cat? What about it being movement that Others can learn and do? In fact, from a social identity point of view, hip hop dance provides something for almost everyone. A piece of identity that is as portable as a digital game player, a BlackBerry, and a personal digital assistant. A remnant of hip hop dance resides in many around the globe, from those who actively or passively shun it to those who consume it directly or indirectly. In this way the connection between hip hop dance and consumption results from the Cabbaging of artifact and historical texts to create the quintessential Patch. It has Bounced from the characterization of the Snake described black man to the Popped Locks embodying resistance to capitalism and the notions promising you can have it your way. More Runnin' Men (and women) have been seen in America and abroad as jobs have gone overseas and as developing geographies are exploited for labor.

Hip hop dance is a black social dance offering texts that deliver strategic and tactical ways of being in the world and remembering worlds past.

Hip hop dance itself is cool, rowdy, defiant, sexy, athletic, smooth, creative. It is also full of meaning—meaning that kind of meaning attributable to ethnographic and cultural contexts. Meanings metabolize in the distribution channel and at points of consumption, when the dance is codified and made into a commodity, used as a medium of value. . . .

Preserving the Art Form

As hip hop dance comes across the screen no tangible named authors of the text exist. But the text is real. It is my view that the history written by the texts of hip hop dance is on the way to being lost in the commercialization, globalization, codification, and commoditization processes. Many have vested interests in these processes. Videographers, product manufacturers, sports cartels, multinational corporations, commercial choreographers, consumers, rappers, and dance studio owners represent only some of the stakeholders who benefit materially from the dissemination of dance texts devoid of meaning and author. The problem with saluting these vested interests, in my opinion, is that doing so limits recognition of hip hop dance as an art form, a written document, and cultural artifact. As it is currently being distributed around the globe, it reminds me of the mass reproduction of, for example, clay pottery art. The purpose of such production is merely for consumption and profit. Those who create the art are often powerless to effect change over the machination. While I may not be able to arrest the processes, I can set forth ideology that sees the dance as text containing historical information that can be read and communicated. These points deserve acknowledgement and preservation, regardless.

Hip hop dance is a black social dance offering texts that deliver strategic and tactical ways of being in the world and remembering worlds past. They contain metaphors and theories about existence and the life of the dancers collectively and individually, and the social fabric we are webbed with. There are macro- and micro-social, political and economic structures of Signification present in these dances begging exploration. For example, in addition to the processes I discussed above, black feminism and hip hop dance have been under-theorized and under-deployed in looking at the currents on which related tactics, metaphors, and theories travel. Moreover, hip hop dance utilizes the choreographed text of US Ebonics [African American vernacular English] for its writing. (I will refer to US Ebonics as Ebonics hereafter for convenience.) However, Ebonics is situated as a spoken language given informal recognition only when one is being a cool consumption cat as such, because now it ain't cool to speak proper American English. Ebonics, though, is a language which nevertheless carries with it Signification. As you can see, there is a lot going on with hip hop dance, and I am just getting started. . . .

Rap and hip hop music have received theoretical attention from many scholars. I could make a laundry list of the different scholars from the fields of cultural, ethnic, African Ameri-

Despite rap music's mass appeal with youth, it has become a subject of controversy. Several critics of rap music charge that its message is violent and antisocial. They believe that rap music provokes violence, especially against police and Whites. [Music historian J.] McDonnell points out that rap music has been blamed for everything from concert muggings to the riots in Los Angeles after the Rodney King verdict. Other critics also charge that rap music promotes racism, sex, drugs, and the degradation of women.

The Positive View of Rap Music

According to [H.] Aldridge and [D.] Carlin, it is often a lack of understanding and knowledge of rap music on the critic's part that is responsible for this kind of negative reaction. A careful analysis of rap music can help demonstrate that not all rap lyrics have negative messages. Aldridge and Carlin point out, "there are numerous examples of songs, which may have a violent tone, but deal with important issues facing the community such as gang violence or single-parent families." Rap music also contains messages about social issues, including promotion of safe sex and traditional family values and prevention of date rapes. Rap music is a reflection of contemporary urban life.

The rap artist serves . . . the role of village oracle, making life comprehensible, defendable, and reachable.

[McDonnell writes that] for African American youth, rap music is a symbol of "hope, increased pride, and self-esteem at a time when any other evidence of the three has been eroded by prevailing social conditions." Dyson says rap music should be taken seriously for its musical, cultural, and social creativity. It expresses "the desire of young black people to reclaim their history, reactivate forms of black radicalism, and contest the powers of despair, hopelessness, and genocide that presently besiege the black community." There is every reason for the existence of rap. The psychological and physical pain and anguish coupled with a sense of injustice and oppression and the need to vent anger and release some of the frustrations have helped spawn the lyrics of rap. The modes of expression of rap music are concerned with the themes of oppression and the need to survive in a hostile environment. According to Rose, rap music contains stories of the "shifting terms of black marginality in contemporary American culture." The cultural and political expressions of rap music serve to empower Black voices from the margins of American society. For many, rap music serves as the "primary cultural, sonic, and linguistic windows on the world."

The Origin of Rap

Rap music has its strong roots in African culture. [Music historian G. Stephens notes that] it manifests several important characteristics of African music and dance such as "percussive performance style," "multiple meter," "call and response," "inner pulse control," and "songs and dances of social allusion/ derision." Similarly, [S.] Miller points out that rap music involves "(re)calling, (re)presenting and (re)constituting African-American histories and experiences as bases for political awarenesses that foreground and (in)form 'Afrocentric' understandings of the conditions that African-Americans now face." In essence, Miller argues that rappers are informed by the African American history and experiences and the artists, in turn, create culture through their lyrics. According to [A.S.] Nelson there are characteristics of rap that "show the persistence of black aesthetic, which is rooted in a dynamic spirituality and the power of rhythm and the spoken word." Similarly, [G.] Smitherman emphasizes the African roots of rap music:

> Rap music is rooted in the Black oral tradition of tonal semantics, narrativising, signification/signifying, the dozens/

playin' the dozens, Africanized syntax, and other communicative practices. . . . The rapper is a postmodern African griot, the verbally gifted storyteller and cultural historian. . . . [Rap artists] decry, for all the world, to hear the deplorable conditions of the hood. . . .

The expressions of rap music are Africa centered as they rely on rhetorical devices such as proverbs, idioms, repetitions, sing-songs, environmental images, metaphors, and folklore, among others. The rap artist serves, as the African griot did, the role of the village oracle, making life comprehensible, defendable, and reachable. Rappers are traditional storytellers in that they are both creators of rhetoric as well as critics of rhetoric. These artists have created with their songs a form of orature that has taken the traditional African forms of communication and redefined and refined them. According to [D.] Toop, rap music originated from the narrative poems called toasts, which are "rhyming stories, often lengthy, which are told mostly amongst me." Toasts are often "violent, scatological, obscene, misogynist" and "have been used for decades to while away time in situations of enforced boredom, whether prison, armed service or streetcorner life." Toop indicates that the origins of rap as a vehicle to recount history and current events can be traced back to the storyteller/historians/musicians of West Africa known as griots. These griots are known for using "gossip and satire" to express their ideas about history and politics.

The Evolution of Rap

Music historians point out that rap music has evolved several times to reach its current stage. According to Dyson, the modern version of rap has gone through three distinct stages. The original form is characterized by "light-hearted banter and boastful self-assertion." The second stage is marked by "social critique" because the message is about "the hurt and horror that make urban life a jungle." This stage of social critique,

Dyson says, can be broken down into three subgenres of gangsta, hardcore, and activist. The third stage of rap is "pluralization," involving "experimentation and coupling of rap with different musical styles (such as soul and rock) and various combinations of elements borrowed from rap's first two stages."

[Musician James] Boyd argues that rap falls into two classes: the popular and the political. The popular form of rap is represented by music that is generally devoid of specific racial content for commercial success, or seeks to reaffirm the dominant culture in the United States. Political rap, on the other hand, is represented by music that "questions the contradictions of the dominant culture and poses an Afrocentric alternative to the cultural dilution of the music by those in search of 'popular' recognition."

The language of urban youth provides a rich field for exploration of a culture within a culture. It is distinctly African centered and grounded in the historical experiences of a people who have been oppressed by their social and political realities and marginalized by their economic and familial conditions. This culture exists alongside an equally African-centered culture, but one with a similar worldview surrounded by oppression and sustained by religion and a transcendent spirit. At times the rhetoric of urban youth appears to be antithetical or dichotomous to its more seasoned counterpart (i.e., gospels and spirituals), but upon closer examination, when using the perspective of Afrocentrism, it becomes clear that where the rhetoric converges, the similarities are remarkable.

Afrocentricity in Rap Music

As stated earlier, this article explores the Afrocentric framework of rhetorical criticism in order to demonstrate its relevance in analyzing the lyrics of rap music. According to [M.] Asante, Afrocentricity implies the "most complete philosophical totalization of the African being-at-the-center of his or her existence." Afrocentricity encompasses all facets of African American life: psychological, political, social, cultural, and economic. For Asante, Afrocentric rhetoric is the "productive thrust of language into the unknown in an attempt to create harmony and balance in the midst of disharmony." [J.L.] Daniel and [G.] Smitherman and [J.D.] Hamlet also underscore the importance of balance and harmony in the African American community, and it is through the creative power of the spoken word, *nommo*, that the African American communicator brings about harmony and balance. . . .

Nommo in Afrocentricity signifies the generative power of the spoken word. The generative function of *nommo* stems from its focus on collectivity, which is the essence of African American spirituality. According to Hamlet, *nommo* is necessary not only to actualize life but also to give people a mastery over things. *Nommo's* presence can be felt in all facets of African American life, including interpersonal, group, public, or mass communication events in which African culture and experiences are fused. It is the quality of *nommo* that has shaped the perception of African Americans to regard a communication event not just as an act where words are spoken in the presence of an audience, but also as a communal experience where those words, songs, dance, and so on give life and meaning to the event.

In the Afrocentric perspective, rhythm, like speech, must coincide with the generative power of the word so that the communicator, word, and audience are all of one accord. Rhythm plays a crucial role in Afrocentric discourse. It is that force that helps to bring about harmony.

Rap Culture's Influence on American Life Is Negative

Rebecca Hagelin

Rebecca Hagelin is the vice president of communications and marketing at the Heritage Foundation. She has written numerous articles published nationally and given hundreds of radio, television, newspaper, and magazine interviews.

"Women and children first."

This famous, selfless cry for the safety of others is best associated with the tragedy of the Titanic, when thousands lost their lives in the frozen waters of the sea so many years ago. Not unlike the rising waters in New Orleans, where the ocean began to fill its natural territory after man-made walls that held it back for so long failed, so the mighty waters of the North Atlantic engulfed the damaged vessel that sought to defy nature's icebergs and open waters. But, unlike New Orleans where dry land was nearby, the Titanic was a lone ship, in the middle of the vast waters, filled with helpless souls who had nowhere to go save too few lifeboats.

The harsh reality that dreadful day in 1912 is that most of the passengers would die, and they knew it. Yet, amid the panic and impending doom, the accounts of survivors remind us of a time when civility and honor were more important to many than survival itself.

So how is it that in fewer than 100 years we have digressed to a society where, when disaster strikes, the story is marked by a display of the worst side of human nature rather than the best?

Gangsta Culture Leads to Crime

Could it be that in a pop culture where the gangsta style is "hip" and is reflected and perpetuated in everything from violent rap and hip-hop music, to the clothing styles, to the language and gestures used in "normal" communication, to the negative attitudes toward females and children, that the "style" isn't just a fashion trend but has actually become a way of life for some? In other words, in a culture where many people dress like gangstas, talk like gangstas, and strut like gangstas, should we be shocked and horrified that they start engaging in gangsta crime when given the opportunity?

I can't help but conclude that if the tragic natural disaster in New Orleans had occurred in a culture that had daily practiced the Golden Rule [of do to others as you would have them do to you], rather than the Gangsta Rot, we would have seen more scenes of neighbors helping neighbors and far fewer scenes of neighbors preying upon neighbors.

Why do we as a nation produce and embrace a pop culture that glorifies rap and hip-hop music?

This is not to say that lawlessness ruled the past week [in September 2005] in New Orleans. The fact is, it didn't. The story of the flood is filled with heroic acts of selflessness, and of desperate neighbor helping desperate neighbor even while death loomed around them. And the amazing generosity from countless Americans—in and near the disaster areas, as well as around the nation—is a testament to the goodness of the American people.

Still, the raping and beating and pillaging and murdering that shocked the world, for many now define not just New Orleans, but American culture.

It's time to ask ourselves a few obvious questions: Why do we as a nation produce and embrace a pop culture that glorifies rap and hip-hop music, that teaches men to prey upon women and engage in senseless violence, and that is now, according to the Kaiser Family Foundation's recent survey on media and youth, the number-one music choice of teenagers from all races and every socio-economic status? Why is it that we produce, en masse, hedonistic movies, television programs, and Internet content? Why is it that we continue to make ever more graphic and violent video games for our children? Why have we allowed such selfish messages to have such a powerful voice in our culture?

Replace Gangsta Values with Civility

Mind you, I'm not advocating government censorship, but rather pleading for social and parental rejection to replace the current proliferation and acceptance of such barbaric and destructive messages.

Other key questions—a bit different but entirely related—for the good people of New Orleans and taxpayers everywhere to ask of Louisiana and federal officials is: Why is it not only common knowledge but also accepted practice that organized crime and gangs hold much of the power and control much of the commerce in New Orleans? Will New Orleans return to business as usual? Or will you uplift the entire community by throwing out the thugs and their vile wares for which New Orleans is infamous? When you think about it, the values of the thugs involved in the post-Katrina crime wave really weren't all that different from those that have flooded sections of New Orleans with societal sewage for years.

Once the immediate danger has passed and the cleanup has begun in earnest, we must, as a nation, ask ourselves many questions. Along with the formal investigations into what went wrong with the local, state and national emergency plans (or lack thereof), we as citizens must also explore how our failure to teach civility, decency and morality gravely compounded the problems of an already horrific disaster.

The stories of the heroic figures of the Titanic and the civility that marked their lives and culture should not be lost. Now is an excellent time to use the lessons of history to build a better future for our children.

Hip-Hop Offers Nothing Uplifting to African American Culture

John H. McWhorter

John H. McWhorter is a senior fellow at the Manhattan Institute for Policy Research and a columnist for the New York Sun. *Known for being an outspoken scholar, he has appeared on news programs such as* Dateline NBC *and has published numerous controversial books including* Winning the Race: Beyond the Crisis in Black America.

Not long ago, I was having lunch in a KFC in Harlem, sitting near eight African-American boys, aged about 14. Since 1) it was 1:30 on a school day, 2) they were carrying book bags, and 3) they seemed to be in no hurry, I assumed they were skipping school. They were extremely loud and unruly, tossing food at one another and leaving it on the floor.

Black people ran the restaurant and made up the bulk of the customers, but it was hard to see much healthy "black community" here. After repeatedly warning the boys to stop throwing food and keep quiet, the manager finally told them to leave. The kids ignored her. Only after she called a male security guard did they start slowly making their way out, tauntingly circling the restaurant before ambling off. These teens clearly weren't monsters, but they seemed to consider themselves exempt from public norms of behavior—as if they had begun to check out of mainstream society.

Rap Music Promotes Antisocial Behavior

What struck me most, though, was how fully the boys' music—hard-edged rap, preaching bone-deep dislike of authority—provided them with a continuing soundtrack to their antiso-

John H. McWhorter, "How Hip-Hop Holds Blacks Back," *City Journal*, summer 2003.

cial behavior. So completely was rap ingrained in their consciousness that every so often, one or another of them would break into cocky, expletive-laden rap lyrics, accompanied by the angular, bellicose gestures typical of rap performance. A couple of his buddies would then join him. Rap was a running decoration in their conversation.

Police forces became marauding invaders in the gangsta-rap imagination.

Many writers and thinkers see a kind of informed political engagement, even a revolutionary potential, in rap and hip-hop. They couldn't be more wrong. By reinforcing the stereotypes that long hindered blacks, and by teaching young blacks that a thuggish adversarial stance is the properly "authentic" response to a presumptively racist society, rap retards black success. . . .

Early rap [began] . . . not as a growl from below but as happy party music. The first big rap hit, the Sugar Hill Gang's 1978 "Rapper's Delight," featured a catchy bass groove that drove the music forward, as the jolly rapper celebrated himself as a ladies' man and a great dancer. Soon, kids across America were rapping along with the nonsense chorus:

I said a hip, hop, the hippie, the
hippie,
to the hip-hip hop, ah you don't
stop
the rock it to the bang bang boogie, say
up jump the boogie,
to the rhythm of the boogie, the
beat.

A string of ebullient raps ensued in the months ahead. At the time, I assumed it was a harmless craze, certain to run out of steam soon.

Rap Turns "Gangsta"

But rap took a dark turn in the early 1980s, as this "bubble gum" music gave way to a "gangsta" style that picked up where blaxploitation [the celebration of the black criminal rebel as a hero] left off. Now top rappers began to write edgy lyrics celebrating street warfare or drugs and promiscuity. Grandmaster Flash's ominous 1982 hit, "The Message," with its chorus, "It's like a jungle sometimes, it makes me wonder how I keep from going under," marked the change in sensibility. It depicted ghetto life as profoundly desolate:

You grow in the ghetto, living second rate
And your eyes will sing a song of
deep hate.
The places you play and where you
stay
Looks like one great big alley way.
You'll admire all the numberbook
takers,
Thugs, pimps and pushers, and the
big money makers.

Music critics fell over themselves to praise "The Message," treating it as the poetry of the streets—as the elite media has characterized hip-hop ever since. The song's grim fatalism struck a chord; twice, I've heard blacks in audiences for talks on race cite the chorus to underscore a point about black victimhood. So did the warning it carried: "Don't push me, 'cause I'm close to the edge," menacingly raps Melle Mel. The ultimate message of "The Message"—that ghetto life is so hopeless that an explosion of violence is both justified and imminent—would become a hip-hop mantra in the years ahead.

Violence and Misogyny Sells

The angry, oppositional stance that "The Message" reintroduced into black popular culture transformed rap from a fad into a multi-billion-dollar industry that sold more than 80 million records in the U.S. in 2002—nearly 13 percent of all recordings sold. To rap producers like Russell Simmons, earlier black pop was just sissy music. He despised the "soft, unaggressive music (and non-threatening images)" of artists like Michael Jackson or Luther Vandross. "So the first chance I got," he says, "I did exactly the opposite."

It's the nastiest rap that sells best, and the nastiest cuts that make a career.

In the two decades since "The Message," hip-hop performers have churned out countless rap numbers that celebrate a ghetto life of unending violence and criminality. Schooly D's "PSK What Does It Mean?" is a case in point:

Copped my pistols, jumped into
the ride.
Got at the bar, copped some flack,
Copped some cheeba-cheeba, it
wasn't wack.
Got to the place, and who did I
see?
A sucka-ass n---a tryin to sound
like me.
Put my pistol up against his
head—
I said, "Sucka-ass n---a, I should
shoot you dead."

The protagonist of a rhyme by KRS-One (a hip-hop star who would later speak out against rap violence) actually pulls the trigger:

Knew a drug dealer by the name of
Peter—
Had to buck him down with my 9
millimeter.

Police forces became marauding invaders in the gangsta-rap imagination. The late West Coast rapper Tupac Shakur expressed the attitude:

Ya gotta know how to shake the
snakes, n---a,
'Cause the police love to break a
n---a,
Send him upstate 'cause they
straight up hate the n---a.

Shakur's anti-police tirade seems tame, however, compared with Ice-T's infamous "Cop Killer":

I got my black shirt on.
I got my black gloves on.
I got my ski mask on.
This shit's been too long.
I got my 12-gauge sawed-off.
I got my headlights turned off.
I'm 'bout to bust some shots off.
I'm 'bout to dust some cops off.
. . .
I'm 'bout to kill me somethin'
A pig stopped me for nuthin'!
Cop killer, better you than me.
Cop killer, f--- police brutality!. . .
Die, die, die pig, die!
F--- the police!. . .
F--- the police yeah!

Rap also began to offer some of the most icily misogynistic music human history has ever known. Here's Schooly D again:

Tell you now, brother, this ain't no
joke,
She got me to the crib, she laid me
on the bed,

I f---ed her from my toes to the
top of my head.
I finally realized the girl was a
whore,
Gave her ten dollars, she asked me
for some more.

Jay-Z's "Is That Yo Bitch?" mines similar themes. . . .

Or, as N.W.A. (an abbreviation of "Niggaz with Attitude")
tersely sums up the hip-hop worldview: "Life ain't nothin' but
bitches and money.". . .

The Worst Are Considered the Best

Of course, not all hip-hop is belligerent or profane—entire
CDs of gang-bangin', police-baiting, woman-bashing invective
would get old fast to most listeners. But it's the nastiest rap
that sells best, and the nastiest cuts that make a career. As I
write, the top ten best-selling hip-hop recordings are 50 Cent
(currently with the second-best-selling record in the nation
among all musical genres), Bone Crusher, Lil' Kim, Fabolous,
Lil' Jon and the East Side Boyz, Cam'ron Presents the Diplo-
mats, Busta Rhymes, Scarface, Mobb Deep, and Eminem. Every one of these groups or performers personifies willful,
staged opposition to society—Lil' Jon and crew even regale us
with a song called "Don't Give a F---"—and every one cel-
ebrates the ghetto as "where it's at." Thus, the occasional duti-
ful songs in which a rapper urges men to take responsibility
for their kids or laments senseless violence are mere garnish.
Keeping the thug front and center has become the quickest
and most likely way to become a star.

No hip-hop luminary has worked harder than Sean "P.
Diddy" Combs, the wildly successful rapper, producer, fashion
mogul, and CEO [chief executive officer] of Bad Boy Records,
to cultivate a gangsta image—so much so that he's blurred the
line between playing the bad boy and really being one. Combs
may have grown up middle-class in Mount Vernon, New York,

and even have attended Howard University for a while, but he's proven he can gang-bang with the worst. Cops charged Combs with possession of a deadly weapon in 1995. In 1999, he faced charges for assaulting a rival record executive. Most notoriously, police charged him that year with firing a gun at a nightclub in response to an insult, injuring three bystanders, and with fleeing the scene with his entourage (including then-pal Jennifer "J. Lo" Lopez). Combs got off, but his young rapper protegé Jamal "Shyne" Barrow went to prison for firing the gun.

How is it progressive to describe life as nothing but "bitches and money"?

Combs and his crew are far from alone among rappers in keeping up the connection between "rap and rap sheet," as critic Kelefa Sanneh artfully puts it. Several prominent rappers, including superstar Tupac Shakur, have gone down in hails of bullets—with other rappers often suspected in the killings. Death Row Records producer Marion "Suge" Knight just finished a five-year prison sentence for assault and federal weapons violations. Current rage 50 Cent flaunts his bullet scars in photos; cops recently arrested him for hiding assault weapons in his car. Of the top ten hip-hop sellers mentioned above, five have had scrapes with the law. In 2000, at least five different fights broke out at the Source Hiphop Awards—intended to be the rap industry's Grammys. The final brawl, involving up to 100 people in the audience and spilling over onto the stage, shut the ceremony down—right after a video tribute to slain rappers. Small wonder a popular rap website goes by the name rapsheet.com.

Praise for Rap Will Ring Hollow Soon

Many fans, rappers, producers, and intellectuals defend hip-hop's violence, both real and imagined, and its misogyny as a revolutionary cry of frustration from disempowered youth. For Simmons, gangsta raps "teach listeners something about the lives of the people who create them and remind them that these people exist." 50 Cent recently told *Vibe* magazine, "Mainstream America can look at me and say, 'That's the mentality of a young man from the 'hood.'" University of Pennsylvania black studies professor Michael Eric Dyson has written a book-length paean to Shakur, praising him for "challenging narrow artistic visions of black identity" and for "artistically exploring the attractions and limits of black moral and social subcultures"—just one of countless fawning treatises on rap published in recent years. The National Council of Teachers of English, recommending the use of hip-hop lyrics in urban public school classrooms (as already happens in schools in Oakland, Los Angeles, and other cities), enthuses that "hip-hop can be used as a bridge linking the seemingly vast span between the streets and the world of academics."

But we're sorely lacking in imagination if in 2003—long after the civil rights revolution proved a success, at a time of vaulting opportunity for African Americans, when blacks find themselves at the top reaches of society and politics—we think that it signals progress when black kids rattle off violent, sexist, nihilistic, lyrics, like Russians reciting [Alexander] Pushkin [who pioneered the use of everyday language in his poems and plays]. Some defended blaxploitation pictures as revolutionary, too, but the passage of time has exposed the silliness of such a contention. . . . Claims about rap's political potential will look equally gestural in the future. How is it progressive to describe life as nothing but "bitches and money"? Or to tell impressionable black kids, who'd find every door open to them if they just worked hard and learned, that blowing a rival's head off is "real"? How helpful is rap's sexism in a community plagued by rampant illegitimacy and an excruciatingly low marriage rate?

The idea that rap is an authentic cry against oppression is all the sillier when you recall that black Americans had lots more to be frustrated about in the past but never produced or enjoyed music as nihilistic as 50 Cent or N.W.A. On the contrary, black popular music was almost always affirmative and hopeful. Nor do we discover music of such violence in places of great misery like Ethiopia or the Congo—unless it's imported American hip-hop.

Given the hip-hop world's reflexive alienation, it's no surprise that its explicit political efforts, such as they are, are hardly progressive. Simmons has founded the "Hip-Hop Summit Action Network" [HSAN] to bring rap stars and fans together in order to forge a "bridge between hip-hop and politics." But HSAN's policy positions are mostly tired bromides. Sticking with the long-discredited idea that urban schools fail because of inadequate funding from the stingy, racist white Establishment, for example, HSAN joined forces with the teachers' union to protest New York mayor [Michael] Bloomberg's proposed education budget for its supposed lack of generosity. HSAN has also stuck it to President [George W.] Bush for invading Iraq. And it has vociferously protested the affixing of advisory labels on rap CDs that warn parents about the obscene language inside. Fighting for rappers' rights to obscenity: that's some kind of revolution!

Don't Dismiss Rap's Power to Influence

Okay, maybe rap isn't progressive in any meaningful sense, some observers will admit; but isn't it just a bunch of kids blowing off steam and so nothing to worry about? I think that response is too easy. With music videos, DVD players, Walkmans [portable music players], the Internet, clothes, and magazines all making hip-hop an accompaniment to a person's entire existence, we need to take it more seriously. In fact, I would argue that it is seriously harmful to the black community.

The rise of nihilistic rap has mirrored the breakdown of community norms among inner-city youth over the last couple of decades. It was just as gangsta rap hit its stride that neighborhood elders began really to notice that they'd lost control of young black men, who were frequently drifting into lives of gang violence and drug dealing. Well into the seventies, the ghetto was a shabby part of town, where, despite unemployment and rising illegitimacy, a healthy number of people were doing their best to "keep their heads above water," as the theme song of the old black sitcom *Good Times* put it.

The attitude and style expressed in the hip-hop "identity" keeps blacks down.

By the eighties, the ghetto had become a ruleless war zone, where black people were their own worst enemies. It would be silly, of course, to blame hip-hop for this sad downward spiral, but by glamorizing life in the "war zone," it has made it harder for many of the kids stuck there to extricate themselves. Seeing a privileged star like Sean Combs behave like a street thug tells those kids that there's nothing more authentic than ghetto pathology, even when you've got wealth beyond imagining.

The attitude and style expressed in the hip-hop "identity" keeps blacks down. Almost all hip-hop, gangsta or not, is delivered with a cocky, confrontational cadence that is fast becoming—as attested to by the rowdies at KFC—a common speech style among young black males. Similarly, the arm-slinging, hand-hurling gestures of rap performers have made their way into many young blacks' casual gesticulations, becoming integral to their self-expression. The problem with such speech and mannerisms is that they make potential employers wary of young black men and can impede a young black's ability to interact comfortably with co-workers and customers. The black community has gone through too much to sacrifice upward mobility to the passing kick of an adversarial hip-hop "identity."

Blacks Promoting Black Stereotypes

On a deeper level, there is something truly unsettling and tragic about the fact that blacks have become the main agents in disseminating debilitating—dare I say racist—images of themselves. Rap guru Russell Simmons claims that "the coolest stuff about American culture—be it language, dress, or attitude—comes from the underclass. Always has and always will." Yet back in the bad old days, blacks often complained—with some justification—that the media too often depicted blacks simply as uncivilized. Today, even as television and films depict blacks at all levels of success, hip-hop sends the message that blacks are . . . uncivilized. I find it striking that the cry-racism crowd doesn't condemn it.

For those who insist that even the invisible structures of society reinforce racism, the burden of proof should rest with them to explain just why hip-hop's bloody and sexist lyrics and videos and the criminal behavior of many rappers *wouldn't* have a powerfully negative effect upon whites' conception of black people.

Sadly, some black leaders just don't seem to care what lesson rap conveys. Consider Savannah [Georgia's] black high schools, which hosted the local rapper Camoflauge as a guest speaker several times before his murder earlier this year [2003]. Here's a representative lyric:

Gimme tha keys to tha car, I'm
ready for war.

When we ride on these n---as
smoke that ass like a 'gar.

Hit your block with a Glock, clear
the set with a Tech. . . .

You think I'm jokin, see if you
laughing when tha pistol be
smokin—

Leave you head split wide open

And you bones get broken. . . .

---

*Hip-hop, with its fantasies of revolution and community
and politics, is more than entertainment. It forms a bedrock of young black identity.*

More than a few of the Concerned Black People inviting
this "artist" to speak to the impressionable youth of Savannah
would presumably be the first to cry out about "how whites
portray blacks in the media."

Avoiding Responsibility

Far from decrying the stereotypes rampant in rap's present-
day blaxploitation, many hip-hop defenders pull the "whitey-
does-it-too" trick. They point to the [Mafia-themed] *Godfather* movies or *The Sopranos* as proof that violence and
vulgarity are widespread in American popular culture, so that
singling out hip-hop for condemnation is simply bigotry. Yet
such a defense is pitifully weak. No one really looks for a way
of life to emulate or a political project to adopt in *The Sopranos*. But for many of its advocates, hip-hop, with its fantasies
of revolution and community and politics, is more than entertainment. It forms a bedrock of young black identity.

Nor will it do to argue that hip-hop isn't "black" music,
since most of its buyers are white, or because the "hip-hop
revolution" is nominally open to people of all colors. That
whites buy more hip-hop recordings than blacks do is hardly
surprising, given that whites vastly outnumber blacks nationwide. More to the point, anyone who claims that rap isn't
black music will need to reconcile that claim with the wide-

spread wariness among blacks of white rappers like Eminem, accused of "stealing our music and giving it back to us."

At 2 AM on the New York subway not long ago, I saw another scene—more dispiriting than my KFC encounter with the rowdy rapping teen—that captures the essence of rap's destructiveness. A young black man entered the car and began to rap loudly—profanely, arrogantly—with the usual wild gestures. This went on for five irritating minutes. When no one paid attention, he moved on to another car, all the while spouting his doggerel. This was what this young black man presented as his message to the world—his oratory, if you will.

Anyone who sees such behavior as a path to a better future—anyone, like Professor Dyson, who insists that hip-hop is an urgent "critique of a society that produces the need for the thug persona"—should step back and ask himself just where, exactly, the civil rights-era blacks might have gone wrong in lacking a hip-hop revolution. They created the world of equality, striving, and success I live and thrive in.

Hip-hop creates nothing.

CHAPTER 2

Does Rap Culture Provide a Positive Outlet for Young People?

Overview: The Emergence of the Hip-Hop Generation

Bakari Kitwana

Bakari Kitwana is a journalist, activist, and political analyst whose commentaries on politics and youth culture have been featured on major television networks such as CNN, FOX News, C-Span, and PBS. He is the author of several books about hip-hop including The Hip-Hop Generation: Young Blacks and the Crisis in African American Culture *and* Why White Kids Love Hip-Hop.

> I've heard enough of [our youth] to know that we ought to be holding them up and sharing with them what we know instead of standing on top of them telling them what they're not doing right. They're doing a lot right and some things wrong. We continue to fail these brilliant, very talented, very creative and courageous young people because they're not saying what our message was. But for Christ's sake . . . we're about to enter the 21st century. Something should be different. And they may be right about some things. —Afeni Shakur, former Black Panther, mother of rapper Tupac Shakur

Ask any young Black American born between 1965 and 1984 where they were on September 13, 1996, and most can tell you. Ask them where they were six months later on March 9, 1997, and you'll get recollections as crystal clear as a baby boomer reminiscing on his or her whereabouts upon hearing of the assassinations of President [John F.] Kennedy, Martin Luther King Jr., or Malcolm X. The September 1996 death of twenty-five-year-old Tupac Shakur was followed by memorials in New York City, Los Angeles, and several cities in between. Likewise the March 1997 death of Christopher Wallace, aka Notorious B.I.G., did not pass without the recognition of his peers. The twenty-four-year-old was commemorated with a statesman-like funeral procession through his old stomping grounds. The deaths of both rap artists fueled record sales of their CDs. Their music and their lives became the subjects of books, college courses, television documentaries, and conference discussions. Killed in a hail of bullets fired by unknown gunmen, both rappers were deemed by countless critics as irresponsible, self-centered thugs who sowed the seeds of their own destruction. Those fans who celebrated their lives were seen as equally irresponsible. But the outpouring of affection was more than simply a fascination with the underworld of rap music and its entertainers. This commemoration of B.I.G. and Pac [Shakur] marked a turning point. Not only had we, the hip-hop generation, come of age, but more importantly, we were conscious of our arrival.

The Hip-Hop Generation

Both rappers, like their peers who saw hope and promise in their short lives, were hip-hop generationers—those young African Americans born between 1965 and 1984 who came of age in the eighties and nineties and who share a specific set of values and attitudes. At the core are our thoughts about family, relationships, child rearing, career, racial identity, race relations, and politics. Collectively, these views make up a complex worldview that has not been concretely defined.

The activism of the younger generation . . . not only fights the power coming from the mainstream politics but is routinely at odds with older-generation activists.

This worldview first began to be expressed in the insightful mid- to late 1980s sociopolitical critiques of rap artists like NWA [Niggaz with Attitude], KRS-One, Poor Righteous

Teachers, Queen Latifah, and others. In the mid-1990s, a handful of young writers such as Carlito Rodriguez, Bonz Malone, Selwyn Hinds, Mimi Valdez, and Scoop Jackson, to name a few, captured this sensibility in their work—although their essays were marginalized in magazines like *The Source*, *Vibe*, and *Rap Pages*. Filmmakers like John Singleton, Albert and Allen Hughes, and Hype Williams (particularly in their 1990s films *Boyz N the Hood*, *Menace II Society*, and *Belly*, respectively), also deftly presented these nuances—as do the youth-specific political concerns articulated almost daily by young activists like Conrad Muhammad, Lisa Sullivan, DeLacy Davis, and Donna Frisby-Greenwood. A delayed response has more recently come out of the academy, most notably in the work of young scholars like historian Robin Kelley and sociologist Mary Pattillo-McCoy.

Collectively, hip-hop-generation writers, artists, filmmakers, activists, and scholars like these laid the foundation for understanding our generation's worldview. Mary Pattillo-McCoy's *Black Picket Fences: Privilege and Peril Among the Black Middle Class*, in comparing middle-class Black Americans to their white counterparts, put it this way:

> We know that middle-class African Americans do not perform as well as whites on standardized tests (in school or in employment); are more likely to be incarcerated for drug offenses; are less likely to marry and more likely to have a child without being married; and are less likely to be working.

Pattillo-McCoy makes clear that even though this Black middle class is about half of the Black population, almost half of it is concentrated in the lower-middle-class region. Pattillo-McCoy also states that this Black middle class is distinguished by its close proximity to the Black working poor. I would add that what Pattillo-McCoy describes above extends to poor and working-class Blacks and not just in comparison to their white counterparts but, more importantly, relative to our parents' generation as well. In reaching these conclusions, Pattillo-McCoy relies on the objective evidence, but this worldview also extends to what we believe.

New Black Youth Culture

Of course, this definition is still fluid as this generation continues to come into its own. But I would further generalize that we, like our white peers, are more likely than our parents' generation to be obsessed with our careers and getting rich quick. For us, achieving wealth, by any means necessary, is more important than most anything else, hence our obsession with the materialistic and consumer trappings of financial success. Central to our identity is a severe sense of alienation between the sexes. Likewise, our perspective on personal relationships and marriage is more likely to take into consideration concerns as diverse as our parents' generation's divorce rates and child support enforcement laws, and we are more likely to be open to family arrangements other than the traditional American family. At the same time, our views of politics, race relations, and racial identity are more likely to have been shaped by [African American activist and Baptist minister] Jesse Jackson's 1984 and 1988 presidential campaigns, the 1992 Los Angeles [race-related] riots, and/or the Million Man March [on Washington, D.C., by thousands of African American men on October 16, 1995]. Our views about safe sex are more likely to have been influenced by Easy E or [basketball star] Magic Johnson's public announcements regarding themselves and HIV/AIDS.

That Black youth share a national culture is nothing new in itself. Black youth culture during the 1920s, the 1930s, and even the 1960s was national in scope. Yet, during each of these periods, Black youth were more likely to derive values and identity from such traditional community institutions as family, church, and school. Despite slight local variations, the passing on of Black culture to the succeeding generation remained orderly and consistent from one Black community to the next. Today the influence of these traditional purveyors of Black culture have largely diminished in the face of powerful and pervasive technological advances and corporate growth. Now media and entertainment such as pop music, film, and fashion are among the major forces transmitting culture to this generation of Black Americans. At the same time, the new Black youth culture cuts across class lines, so that whether one is middle class, coming of age in a suburban or rural setting, college-bound, or a street-wise urban dweller, what it means to be young and Black has been similarly redefined. As such, the defining values of this generation's worldview have taken a dramatic turn away from our parents' generation.

The Generation Gap

For our parents' generation, the political ideals of civil rights and Black power are central to their worldview. Our parents' generation placed family, spirituality, social responsibility, and Black pride at the center of their identity as Black Americans. They, like their parents before them, looked to their elders for values and identity. The core set of values shared by a large segment of the hip-hop generation—Black America's generation X—stands in contrast to our parents' worldview. For the most part, we have turned to ourselves, our peers, global images and products, and the new realities we face for guidance. In the process, the values and attitudes described above anchor our worldview.

New ways of relieving current forms of oppression can be implemented only when younger and older generations do so together.

Our parents' values maintain a strong presence within our worldview. But in cases where the old and the new collide, the old—more often than not—is superseded by the new. For example, Black pride is still an important part of this generation's identity. In fact, the hip-hop generation has embraced the idea of Blackness in ways that parallel the Black consciousness raising of the late 1960s and early 1970s. The popularization of the Afrocentric movement from the late 1980s through the 1990s, pro-Black lyrics on the contemporary rap scene, as well as traditional hairstyles (dread-locks and braids, for example) adopted by many hip-hop generationers all speak to this. Regardless of whether this is a brand of hard-core nationalism or a lukewarm, flash-in-the-pan bou-gie [aspiring to be upper class] nationalism, the fact remains that when many hip-hop generation youth have to choose between personal financial success at the expense of what the older generation considers communal cultural integrity, individual gain generally comes first.

Expressions of the Hip-Hop Generation

It is important to distinguish this worldview from hip-hop culture, the youth-oriented lifestyle that birthed rap music. Certainly, the commercialization of rap music expanded the definition of hip-hop culture beyond the four elements (graffiti, break dancing, dj-ing, rap music) to include verbal language, body language, attitude, style, and fashion. By contrast, the new Black youth culture is expressed both publicly and privately in myriad ways. You see the street culture manifestation of this in "'hood" films and hip-hop magazines like *The Source* as much as in rap music and hip-hop culture. You see it in the defiant attitude and disposition of our generation's professional athletes and entertainers like [basketball star] Allen Iverson, [football player] Ray Lewis, [boxer] Mike Tyson, [football player] Randy Moss, and [baseball player] Albert Belle. You see it in the activism of the younger generation, which not only fights the power coming from the mainstream politics but is routinely at odds with older-generation activists like Jesse Jackson, Kweisi Mfume, and Al

Sharpton. You see it coming from happy-to-be-middle-class-themed magazines like *Honey* and *Savoy* as well as like-minded, youth-oriented television programming such as MTV and on-line publications like BET.com. . . .

"Each generation," writes [decolonization activist] Frantz Fanon in *The Wretched of the Earth*—the bible for activists in our parents' generation and a source often cited in the nostalgic search for deeper values within our own—"out of relative obscurity, must discover their mission, fulfill it or betray it." Now more than ever these divided generations must begin to understand the ways that the new Black youth culture both empowers and undermines Black America. As brilliant a moment in history as the civil rights and Black power eras were, the older generation must realize they cannot claim any real victory if the hip-hop generation cannot build significantly on those gains. The younger generation must understand that no matter how grand our individual achievements (achievements built on the gains from past struggles), they mean very little if we cannot overcome at least some of the major social obstacles of our time, leaving a formidable foundation on which the next generation can stand strong. As long as the older generation fails to understand the new Black youth culture in all of its complexities, and as long as the younger generation fails to see its inherent contradictions, we cannot as a community address the urgent crises now upon us, particularly those facing Black American youth. New ways of relieving current forms of oppression can be implemented only when the younger and older generations do so together. Our collective destiny demands it.

The rags-to-riches rap careers, the lyrics, and very lifestyles of Tupac and B.I.G. epitomize the new Black youth culture. Like their lives and deaths, each of these elements informs the worldview of our generation and speaks to our attitudes about all aspects of life from sex, love, and family to community, education, and future possibilities. This new Black youth culture raises some critical questions: how has Black America changed, what new circumstances and conditions have affected its evolution, and finally, what is the legacy of that culture at the dawn of the millennium? If Pac and B.I.G. are to be martyrs for the hip-hop generation, let them be martyrs in beginning an intergenerational movement to answer these questions and resolve those problems that threaten to undermine the very fabric and future of Black America.

Some Rap Music Promotes Political Empowerment for Minority Youth

Yvonne Bynoe

A cultural critic and political analyst, Yvonne Bynoe is the pub-
lisher of Full Disclosure: The Business of Hip-Hop, *a newslet-*
ter dedicated to empowering rap artists and entrepreneurs in the
business side of the music industry.

While rap remains mired in controversy, controversies regarding Black music and its artists are nothing new.
African-American music that came from the streets has always
embarrassed the Black bourgeoisie, who wanted art to "uplift
the race." During the Harlem Renaissance [the black cultural
and social movement of the 1920s and '30s], this group dis-
liked Negro spirituals, detested the blues, and hated the now-
lionized jazz because it was too closely associated with the
demimonde [a class of people of low reputation]. The major
distinction between that era and today is that then, in segregated America, Black people's dirty laundry was aired only
among family; now in this age of global media, the entire
world gets a peek. As such, the ashamed Black middle class
are now being joined by frightened White suburbanites whose
rebellious children are buying an estimated 70 percent of the
rap music consumed in this country.

Rap is American, but with a defiant shout. The sexism,
violence, and nihilism that are depicted in rap music are that
which exist in this country. Rap music is by nature confrontational and at times vulgar, but these characteristics do not negate it as a true musical art form. Critics like jazz musician
Delfayo Marsalis say that rap music is not art because art

"transcends life" rather than imitating it. But the concept of art transcending life negates the power and importance of everyday experiences, beliefs, and judgments. Professor Maulena Karenga's definition of art speaks to those who value realism, characterizing art as: "Cultural production informed by standards of creativity and beauty and inspired by and reflective of a people's life-experiences and life-aspirations." Karenga's definition, while utilitarian, provides space for art that is based in the immediate present—art that forces us to examine our environment and circumstances. Rap music is very much expressive of the lives of people who live in the 'hood and also those who are invisible in society. As is the case with all art, not every rap song is a masterpiece or even particularly significant to the genre, but others are priceless.

[Director] Spike Lee, in his movie *Bamboozled*, slyly alludes to rap artists being the equivalent of modern-day minstrels, a sentiment echoed by many Black Americans, including rap artist Chuck D. To an extent the critics are right; we have been bamboozled by the entertainment industry. Similar to the recruitment of [*Bamboozled* characters] Mantan and Eat 'n' Sleep to the New Millennium Minstrel show, annually a succession of young, undereducated Black men, seeking to escape dead end jobs or the streets are welcomed by the music industry. The record companies encourage these young people to tell their ghetto tales (real or imagined) in the crudest fashion for predominately White rap CD buyers. Right now the most successful rap artists can become multimillionaires by being vulgar, misogynistic, and antisocial. More important, there are Black executives who are promoting this type of rap music to impressionable youth; Black video directors who come up with scurrilous video concepts; young Black women who beg to disrobe for these videos; and a population of Black adults who, through their silence, are accomplices to this cultural hoodwinking. Critics, rather than solely blaming the rap artists, would be better served to address the corporate minstrel makers and the circumstances that produce willing coons: poverty, ghetto conditions, unemployment, and unequal opportunities.

Industry Control

If there is a problem within rap music and Hip Hop culture, it is a lack of diversity, rather than a need for censorship. Like the rest of Black America, the world of Hip Hop is not a monolith, yet all too often Hip Hop is only represented by young Black males with gold teeth, wearing baggy pants and shouting obscenities, and libidinous young Black women shakin' their asses. What the music industry has done through rap music is to frame the "authentic" Black American not as a complex, educated, or even creative individual, but as a "real n---a" who has ducked bullets, worked a triple beam, and done at least one bid in prison. This image, along with that of scantily clad women, is then transmitted worldwide as a testament of who Black Americans are. This means that corporate entertainment entities have no vested interest in seeing that rap artists advance themselves creatively or intellectually. As [African American educator and writer] W.E.B. Du Bois asserts in "Color and Democracy", the colonizer's "sudden interest . . . in the preservation of native culture" and its vernacular is a way to keep primitives from "modern cultural patterns." In essence, if the media image of rap music and Hip Hop is radically altered, then the societal image of an "authentic" Black American would also have to be radically altered.

While commercial rap artists extol the virtues of conspicuous consumption, conscious rap artists discuss empowerment through politics and knowledge.

Unlike the early days of rap music, when all types of styles and messages coexisted, today corporate entertainment only allows one rap type at a time. With an extremely narrowed concept of rap, there has developed a schism within the Hip Hop community as to how it should be represented and by whom. Although it is a drastic over-simplification of the genre, for this brief discussion, there have become essentially two camps of rap devotees: the ones who favor so-called "conscious rap," which caters to an underground audience, and those who favor the glitzy, "commercial rap," which is played incessantly on urban radio. These terms themselves are almost misnomers since a conscious artist can become commercial, although the converse is rarely true. This was the case with conscious rap artist Lauryn Hill, who became a commercial artist. In 1999, Hill became the first woman ever to win five Grammy awards including, "Album of the Year," for *The MisEducation of Lauryn Hill.*; Hill had been nominated for ten Grammys that year. Moreover, the terms are subjective since many of the conscious rap artists use the word *n---a*, use profanity, smoke weed, and are unwed parents and some commercial artists are reflective and produce thought-provoking work. At best the terms are shorthand, with *conscious* meaning socially and politically aware and *commercial* meaning materialistic and wanton. . . .

Conscious Rap

While commercial rap artists extol the virtues of conspicuous consumption, conscious rap artists discuss empowerment through politics and knowledge. Among those flying the flag of conscious Hip Hop is Common (Lonnie Rashid Lynn). With the release of his fourth album titled, *Like Water for Chocolate,* after the Mexican novel, Common has finally found mainstream success. Prior to the album's release Common was probably best known for his hats, being from Chicago, and his rap battle with former NWA [Niggaz with Attitude] member Ice Cube, which resulted in Common's retaliatory single, "For the Bitch in Yoo." Generally, Common's songs talk about gaining self-awareness in a society consumed by self-destructive principles. His topics have included abortion, the deceit of the music industry, sexual restraint, the Black family, and the direction of Hip Hop. On this latest album Common includes tributes to Nigerian artist Fela Kuti and political exile Assata Shakur whom he went to Cuba to meet. "A Song for Assata" recounts her capture by police and her exile to Cuba. Common may be conscious but he is not totally politically correct. He has been accused of homophobia for his use of the term *faggot* in his song, "Dooinit." Though he denies the charges of homophobia, he admits that he did use the term as a pejorative. Common, however, is the first to admit that he is evolving as a man and as an artist.

Mos Def (Dante Beze) is the current darling of the conscious Hip Hop world. The Brooklyn native and his partner Talib Kweli stepped into the forefront with the release of their album, *Mos Def and Talib Kweli Are . . . Black Star* in 1998. Called Marcus Garveyesque [reminiscent of black nationalism leader Garvey] by some, this album provided desperate fans with a new source of smart rap music. A year later, Mos released his solo album, *Black on Both Sides*, which was certified platinum. This album displayed not only Mos's versatility as a trained musician, but also his insightful Black Power politics. Mos's activism however goes beyond rhyming. Reminiscent of KRS-One's Stop the Violence effort nearly a decade before, Mos organized a collective of rap artists to record the *Hip Hop for Respect* CD and video. *Hip Hop for Respect* protested the death of African immigrant Amadou Diallo, shot by four policemen in New York City. The proceeds from the CD went to the Hip Hop For Respect Foundation, a nonprofit organization that encourages entertainment industry professionals to become involved in their fans' communities. To that end, Mos Def and Talib Kweli purchased Nkiru Books in Brooklyn, which was on the verge of bankruptcy. Mos is also an actor who has appeared as a member of the Mau Maus rap group in *Bamboozled*, in a VISA commercial, on an episode of the television show *NYPD Blue*, and in Suzan Lori-Park's Pulitzer Prize–winning play, *Top Dog/Underdog*. Like Lauryn Hill, Mos is a conscious rap artist poised to become commercial.

Dead Prez see Hip Hop as a commodity in the world of global capitalism, but one that can have social value to people of color if artists are willing to retake control of it.

The most political rap artists since Public Enemy may be the duo Dead Prez. Many of Dead Prez's lyrical influences come from the Black Power movement. Identifying with the history of Black political struggle is the core of the duo's philosophy, On their first album, *Let's Be Free*, many of the songs outline the overlooked history of the struggle of Black people, with the listener being urged to immediately get involved with progressive political projects. Challenging the hypocrisy of much rap music and Hip Hop culture, M-1 has been quoted as saying

> Hip Hop today is programmed by the ruling class. It is not the voice of African or Latino or oppressed youth. It is a puppet voice for the ruling class, that tells us to act like those people who are oppressing us. Who's to blame? The schools, the media, capitalism, and colonialism are totally responsible for what Hip Hop is and what it has become. But we didn't intend on that—Hip Hop was a voice just like the drum, the oral tradition of our people.

Dead Prez see Hip Hop as a commodity in the world of global capitalism, but one that can have social value to people of color if artists are willing to retake control of it. The duo reconcile their business alliance with Loud Records by deeming it a strategic means of getting "their" message out to as many people as possible, thus being able to create more radicals

Censorship is one of the evils that Dead Prez continues to fight. Rawkus Records deleted their verse for the *Hip Hop for*

Respect CD. The duo's record company, Loud Records, chose to slap a sticker over the cover photo *Let's Get Free*, which shows youths in Soweto [South Africa], guns held high, celebrating a victory over police. Additionally, video outlets such as BET and MTV reportedly asked Loud Records to edit the video for the Dead Prez's second single, "They Schools." The clip in question blasts the U.S. educational system for its miseducation of people of color with such no-nonsense images as the duo being hung with nooses and the burning of textbooks. The artists have also been banned from several venues in New York City because of their political messages.

Art Supporting Politics

Although individual artists and groups are political, a long-standing criticism of Hip Hop by the civil rights community is that it has not generated a sustainable political movement. The criticism is somewhat illogical since overt political engagement was not Hip Hop's raison d'etre [reason for existence]. Rap music began as community entertainment and any political function was largely subtextual. Moreover, Hip Hop seeks to define a specific group reality within our society, while politics seeks to define or redefine society at large.

In basic terms, rap artists raising awareness about police brutality through a song or performance is rap/Hip Hop, but activists and legislators forcing changes in police department procedures or the laws used to prosecute corrupt cops is politics.

Thus, before any large-scale movement can be contemplated, the post-civil rights generation will first have to build a viable political apparatus that incorporates the cultural expression Hip Hop. The model for such a structure would be the relationship between the Black Power movement and the Black Arts movement. The former outlined a political ideology, while the latter used cultural expressions to support the Black Power principles.

Rap music entered the overt political realm in 1982 when Grandmaster Flash and the Furious Five rapped about life in the ghetto in "The Message." By the late 1980s the commercial success of politically conscious rap artists had caused the media to identify them, rather than young activists, organizers, and legislators, as the political spokesmen of the Hip Hop generation. Unfortunately the inability of these insightful artists to organize a political movement underscores the contradiction of so-called Hip Hop politics. If the Hip Hop community ever spawns a movement it will because it galvanizes around a particular issue or set of issues that require legislative redress like the Bay Area's Third Eye Movement did in 2000 in its fight against Proposition 21 [which increased penalties for crimes committed by youths]. Moreover, in so doing, the participants would make clear distinctions between culture and politics. In this movement rap artists would use their celebrity to raise public awareness, but the leaders would be full-time community organizers, activists, and emerging politicians. . . .

[African American writer] James Baldwin is attributed with saying, "To be conscious in America is to be in a constant state of rage." For those of us who are conscious, all of this is about more than Hip Hop. Hip Hop is simply the metaphor for our lives. If our elders give up on Hip Hop, then they've given up on us. If we give up on Hip Hop, then we've given up on ourselves. Despite its dynamism, Hip Hop can be no more than what we are capable of saying or allow to be said.

Teens Identify with the Broken Homes Portrayed in Rap Music

Mary Eberstadt

Mary Eberstadt is a fellow at the Hoover Institution and a consulting editor to its bimonthly journal Policy Review. *She is the author of several books, including* Home-Alone America: The Hidden Toll of Day Care, Behavioral Drugs and Other Parent Substitutes.

W hat is the overall influence of this deafening, foul, and often vicious-sounding stuff on children and teenagers? This is a genuinely important question, and serious studies and articles, some concerned particularly with current music's possible link to violence, have lately been devoted to it. In 2000, the American Academy of Pediatrics, the American Medical Association, the American Psychological Association, and the American Academy of Child & Adolescent Psychiatry all weighed in against contemporary lyrics and other forms of violent entertainment before Congress with a first-ever "Joint Statement on the Impact of Entertainment Violence on Children."

What Today's Music Says About Today's Teens

Nonetheless, this is not my focus here. Instead, I would like to turn that logic about influence upside down and ask this question: What is it about today's music, violent and disgusting though it may be, that resonates with so many American kids?

As the reader can see, this is a very different way of inquiring about the relationship between today's teenagers and their music. The first question asks what the music does to adolescents; the second asks what it tells us about them. To answer that second question is necessarily to enter the roiling emotional waters in which that music is created and consumed—in other words, actually to listen to some of it and read the lyrics.

As it turns out, such an exercise yields a fascinating and little understood fact about today's adolescent scene. If yesterday's rock was the music of abandon, today's is that of abandonment. The odd truth about contemporary teenage music—the characteristic that most separates it from what has gone before—is its compulsive insistence on the damage wrought by broken homes, family dysfunction, checked-out parents, and (especially) absent fathers. Papa Roach, Everclear, Blink-182, Good Charlotte, Eddie Vedder and Pearl Jam, Kurt Cobain and Nirvana, Tupac Shakur, Snoop Doggy Dogg [currently known as Snoop Dogg], Eminem—these and other singers and bands, all of them award-winning top-40 performers who either are or were among the most popular icons in America, have their own generational answer to what ails the modern teenager. Surprising though it may be to some, that answer is: dysfunctional childhood. Moreover, and just as interesting, many bands and singers explicitly link the most deplored themes in music today—suicide, misogyny, and drugs—with that lack of a quasi-normal, intact-home personal past.

To put this perhaps unexpected point more broadly, during the same years in which progressive-minded and politically correct adults have been excoriating Ozzie and Harriet [TV characters representing the traditional family] as an artifact of 1950s-style oppression, many millions of American teenagers have enshrined a new generation of music idols whose shared generational signature in song after song is to rage about what not having had a nuclear family has done to them. This is quite a fascinating puzzle of the times. The self-perceived emotional damage scrawled large across contemporary music may not be statistically quantifiable, but it is nonetheless among the most striking of all the unanticipated consequences of our home-alone world. . . .

Where Is Daddy?

Even less recognized than the white music emphasis on broken homes and the rest of the dysfunctional themes is that the popular black-dominated genres, particularly hip-hop/rap, also reflect themes of abandonment, anger, and longing for parents. Interestingly enough, this is true of particular figures whose work is among the most adult deplored.

Once again, when it comes to the deploring part, critics have a point. It is hard to imagine a more unwanted role model (from the parental point of view) than the late Tupac Shakur. A best-selling gangsta rapper who died in a shoot-out in 1996 at age 25 (and the object of a 2003 documentary called *Tupac: Resurrection*), Shakur was a kind of polymath [a person of encyclopedic learning] of criminality. In the words of a *Denver Post* review of the movie, "In a perfect circle of life imitating art originally meant to imitate life, Shakur in 1991 began a string of crimes that he alternately denied and reveled in. He claimed Oakland [California] police beat him up in a jaywalking arrest, later shot two off-duty cops, assaulted a limo driver and video directors, and was shot five times in a robbery." Further, "At the time of his drive-by murder in Las Vegas, he was out on bail pending appeal of his conviction for sexual abuse of a woman who charged him with sodomy in New York."

Perhaps not surprising, Shakur's songs are riddled with just about every unwholesome trend that a nervous parent can name; above all they contain incitements to crime and violence (particularly against the police) and a misogyny so pronounced that his own mother, executive producer of the movie, let stand in the film a statement of protesting C. De-

Lores Tucker that "African-American women are tired of being called ho's, bitches and sluts by our children."

Growing up fatherless might help to explain why Shakur is an icon not only to many worse-off teenagers from the ghetto, but also to many better-off suburban ones.

Yet Shakur—who never knew his father and whose mother, a long time drug addict, was arrested for possession of crack when he was a child—is provocative in another, quite overlooked way: He is the author of some of the saddest lyrics in the hip-hop/gangsta-rap pantheon, which is saying quite a lot. To sophisticated readers familiar with the observations about the breakup of black families recorded several decades ago in the Moynihan Report [a 1965 Senate report headed by Daniel Patrick Moynihan identifying the legacies of slavery, urbanization, discrimination, and matriarchy as reasons why many black families suffer crises] and elsewhere, the fact that so many young black men grow up without fathers may seem so well established as to defy further comment. But evidently some young black men—Shakur being one—see things differently. In fact, it is hard to find a rapper who does not sooner or later invoke a dead or otherwise long-absent father, typically followed by the hope that he will not become such a man himself. Or there is the flip side of that unintended bow to the nuclear family, which is the hagiography [idealization] in some rappers' lyrics of their mothers.

Rap Songs of Dysfunction

In a song called "Papa'z Song Lyrics," Shakur opens with the narrator imagining his father showing up after a long absence, resulting in an expletive-laden tirade. The song then moves to a lacerating description of growing up fatherless that might help to explain why Shakur is an icon not only to many worse-off teenagers from the ghetto, but also to many better-off suburban ones. Here is a boy who "had to play catch by myself," who prays: "Please send me a pops before puberty."

The themes woven together in this song—anger, bitterness, longing for family, misogyny as the consequence of a world without fathers—make regular appearances in some other rappers' lyrics, too. One is Snoop Doggy Dogg, perhaps the preeminent rapper of the 1990s. Like Shakur and numerous other rappers, his personal details cause many a parent to shudder; since his childhood he has been arrested for a variety of crimes, including cocaine possession (which resulted in three years of jail service), accomplice to murder (for which he was acquitted), and, most recently, marijuana possession. ("It's not my job to stop kids doing the wrong thing, it's their parents' job," he once explained to a reporter.) In a song called "Mama Raised Me," sung with Soulja Slim, Snoop Doggy Dogg offers this explanation of how troubled pasts come to be: "It's probably pop's fault how I ended up/Gangbangin'; crack slangin'; not givin' a f----."

> *The fact that child abandonment is also a theme in hip-hop might help explain . . . how this particular music moved from the fringes of black entertainment to the very center of Everyteenager mainstream.*

Another black rapper who returned repeatedly to the theme of father abandonment is Jay-Z, also known as Shawn Carter, whose third and break-through album, *Hard Knock Life*, sold more than 500,000 copies. He also has a criminal history (he says he had been a cocaine dealer) and a troubled family history, which is reflected in his music. In an interview with MTV.com about his latest album, the reporter explained: "Jay and his father had been estranged until earlier this year. [His father] left the household and his family's life (Jay has an older brother and two sisters) when Shawn was just 12 years old. The separation had served as a major 'block' for Jay over the years. . . . His most vocal tongue lashing toward his dad was on the *Dynasty: Roc la Familia* cut 'Where Have You Been,' where he rapped 'F--- you very much/You showed me the worst kind of pain.'"

The fact that child abandonment is also a theme in hip-hop might help explain what otherwise appears as a commercial puzzle—namely, how this particular music moved from the fringes of black entertainment to the very center of the Everyteenager mainstream. There can be no doubt about the current social preeminence of these black- and ghetto-dominated genres in the lives of many better-off adolescents, black and white. As Donna Britt wrote in a *Washington Post* column noting hip-hop's ascendancy, "In modern America, where urban based hip hop culture dominates music, fashion, dance and, increasingly, movies and TV, these kids are trendsetters. What they feel, think and do could soon play out in a middle school—or a Pottery Barn–decorated bedroom—near you."

Eminem: Reasons for Rage

A final example of the rage in contemporary music against irresponsible adults—perhaps the most interesting—is that of genre-crossing bad-boy rap superstar Marshall Mathers or Eminem (sometime stage persona "Slim Shady"). Of all the names guaranteed to send a shudder down the parental spine, his is probably the most effective. In fact, Eminem has single-handedly, if inadvertently, achieved the otherwise ideologically impossible: He is the object of a vehemently disapproving public consensus shared by the National Organization for Women [NOW], the Gay & Lesbian Alliance Against Defamation, [conservative politician and writer] William J. Bennett, Lynne Cheney [wife of Vice President Dick Cheney and a scholar and author], [conservative news commentator] Bill O'Reilly, and a large number of other social conservatives as well as feminists and gay activists. In sum, this rapper—"as harmful to America as any al Qaeda fanatic," in O'Reilly's opinion—unites adult polar opposites as perhaps no other single popular entertainer has done.

Eminem also repeatedly centers his songs on the crypto-traditional notion that children need parents and that not having them has made all hell break loose.

There is small need to wonder why. Like other rappers, Eminem mines the shock value and gutter language of rage, casual sex, and violence. Unlike the rest, however, he appears to be a particularly attractive target of opprobrium [contempt] for two distinct reasons. One, he is white and therefore politically easier to attack. (It is interesting to note that black rappers have not been targeted by name anything like Eminem has.) Perhaps even more important, Eminem is one of the largest commercially visible targets for parental wrath. Wildly popular among teenagers these last several years, he is also enormously successful in commercial terms. Winner of numerous Grammys and other music awards and a perpetual nominee for many more, he has also been critically (albeit reluctantly) acclaimed for his acting performance in the autobiographical 2003 movie *8 Mile*. For all these reasons, he is probably the preeminent rock/rap star of the last several years, one whose singles, albums, and videos routinely top every chart. His 2002 album, *The Eminem Show*, for example, was easily the most successful of the year, selling more than 7.6 million copies.

This remarkable market success, combined with the intense public criticism that his songs have generated, makes the phenomenon of Eminem particularly intriguing. Perhaps more than any other current musical icon, he returns repeatedly to the same themes that fuel other success stories in contemporary music: parental loss, abandonment, abuse, and subsequent child and adolescent anger, dysfunction, and violence (including self-violence). Both in his raunchy lyrics as well as in *8 Mile*, Mathers's own personal story has been parlayed many times over: the absent father, the troubled mother living in a trailer park, the series of unwanted maternal boyfriends, the protective if impotent feelings toward a younger sibling (in the movie, a baby sister; in real life, a younger brother), and the fine line that a poor, ambitious, and unguided young man might walk between catastrophe and success. Mathers plumbs these and related themes with a verbal savagery that leaves most adults aghast.

Eminem's Family Ideal

Yet Eminem also repeatedly centers his songs on the crypto-traditional notion that children need parents and that not having them has made all hell break loose. In the song "8 Mile" from the movie soundtrack, for example, the narrator studies his little sister as she colors one picture after another of an imagined nuclear family, failing to understand that "mommas got a new man." "Wish I could be the daddy that neither one of us had," he comments. Such wistful lyrics juxtapose oddly and regularly with Eminem's violent other lines. Even in one of his most infamous songs, "Cleaning Out My Closet (Mama, I'm Sorry)," what drives the vulgar narrative is the insistence on seeing abandonment from a child's point of view. "My faggot father must have had his panties up in a bunch/'Cause he split. I wonder if he even kissed me good-bye."

This is not the expression of random misogyny but, rather, of primal rage over alleged maternal abdication and abuse.

As with other rappers, the vicious narrative treatment of women in some of Eminem's songs is part of this self-conception as a child victim. Contrary to what critics have intimated, the misogyny in current music does not spring from nowhere; it is often linked to the larger theme of having been abandoned several times—left behind by father, not nurtured by mother, and betrayed again by faithless womankind. One of the most violent and sexually aggressive songs in the last few years is "Kill You" by the popular metal band known as Korn. Its violence is not directed toward just any woman or even toward the narrator's girlfriend; it is instead a song about an abusive stepmother whom the singer imagines going back to rape and murder.

Similarly, Eminem's most shocking lyrics about women are not randomly dispersed; they are largely reserved for his mother and ex-wife, and the narrative pose is one of despising them for not being better women—in particular, better mothers. The worst rap directed at his own mother is indeed gut-wrenching: "But how dare you try to take what you didn't help me to get?/You selfish bitch, I hope you f------ burn in hell for this shit!" It is no defense of the gutter to observe the obvious: This is not the expression of random misogyny but, rather, of primal rage over alleged maternal abdication and abuse.

Bad Parents Make Bad Teens

Another refrain in these songs runs like this: Today's teenagers are a mess, and the parents who made them that way refuse to get it. In one of Eminem's early hits, for example, a song called "Who Knew," the rapper pointedly takes on his many middle- and upper-middle-class critics to observe the contradiction between their reviling him and the parental inattention that feeds his commercial success. "What about the make-up you allow your 12 year-old daughter to wear?" he taunts.

This same theme of AWOL [absent without leave] parenting is rapped at greater length in another award-nominated 2003 song called "Sing for the Moment," whose lyrics and video would be recognized in an instant by most teenagers in America. That song spells out Eminem's own idea of what connects him to his millions of fans—a connection that parents, in his view, just don't (or is that won't?) understand. It details the case of one more "problem child" created by "His f------ dad walkin' out." "Sing for the Moment," like many other songs of Eminem's, is also a popular video. The "visuals" show clearly what the lyrics depict—hordes of disaffected kids, with flashbacks to bad home lives, screaming for the singer who feels their pain. It concludes by rhetorically turning away from the music itself and toward the emotionally desperate teenagers who turn out for this music by the millions. If the demand of all those empty kids wasn't out there, the narrator says pointedly, then rappers wouldn't be supplying it the way they do.

Entertainers . . . blame the absent, absentee, and generally inattentive adults whose deprived and furious children . . . have catapulted today's singers to fame.

If some parents still don't get it—even as their teenagers elbow up for every new Eminem CD and memorize his lyrics with psalmist devotion—at least some critics observing the music scene have thought to comment on the ironies of all this. In discussing *The Marshall Mathers LP* in 2001 for *Music Box*, a daily online newsletter about music, reviewer John Metzger argued, "Instead of spewing the hate that he is so often criticized of doing, Eminem offers a cautionary tale that speaks to our civilization's growing depravity. Ironically, it's his teenage fans who understand this, and their all-knowing parents that miss the point." Metzger further specified "the utter lack of parenting due to the spendthrift necessity of the two-income family."

That insight raises the overlooked fact that in one important sense Eminem and most of the other entertainers quoted here would agree with many of today's adults about one thing: The kids aren't all right out there after all. Recall, for just one example, [alternative rock artist] Eddie Vedder's rueful observation about what kind of generation would make him or [Vedder's contemporary] Kurt Cobain its leader. Where parents and entertainers disagree is over who exactly bears responsibility for this moral chaos. Many adults want to blame the people who create and market today's music and videos. Entertainers, Eminem most prominently, blame the absent, absentee, and generally inattentive adults whose deprived and furious children (as they see it) have catapulted today's singers to fame. (As he puts the point in one more in-your-face response to parents: "Don't blame me when lil' Eric jumps off of the terrace / You shoulda been watchin him—apparently you ain't parents.")

The spectacle of a foul-mouthed bad-example rock icon instructing the hardworking parents of America in the art of child-rearing is indeed a peculiar one, not to say ridiculous. The single mother who is working frantically because she must and worrying all the while about what her 14-year-old is listening to in the headphones is entitled to a certain fury over lyrics like those. In fact, to read through most rap lyrics is to wonder which adults or political constituencies wouldn't take offense. Even so, the music idols who point the finger away from themselves and toward the emptied-out homes of America are telling a truth that some adults would rather not hear. In this limited sense at least, Eminem is right.

Young People Should Not Emulate Rappers

Canadian Press

Founded in 1917, the Canadian Press is Canada's national news reporting agency. The Canadian Press provides real-time text, photos, audio, graphics, video, and online services to newspapers, broadcasters, publishers, Web sites, wireless carriers, cable companies, and government and corporate clients.

Many black students today are failing in school on purpose because peer pressure via media images has convinced them that smart equals white and that it's cool to become pimps or "video ho's" says pre-eminent African-American filmmaker Spike Lee.

And Lee told an audience comprised largely of Ontario [Canada] university students that people can vote with their pocketbooks to convince artists, record companies and media conglomerates like Viacom that the images in today's music videos or lyrics in gangsta rap are unacceptable.

"As African-Americans we let artists slide," Lee said in the Monday night [March 14, 2005] speech. "(But) those days are over. I think that we have to start to hold people accountable."

Lee was invited to speak in Toronto by the Ryerson University student administrative council to help mark the International Day For the Elimination of Racial Discrimination on March 21.

Make Rap Artists Accountable

While known for his outspokenness, especially on issues of race, Lee seemed to aim his heavy guns at fellow black artists. He said that while he wasn't calling for a boycott, the father now of a 10-year-old girl said he could no longer listen to the music of R. Kelly because he saw the bootleg video of the rapper with some underage females.

"These artists talk about 'ho this, bitch this, skank this' and all the other stuff. They're talking about all our mothers, all our sisters. They're talking about their own mothers, grandmothers."

"You have to have knowledge of self and knowledge of history. Because if you had that you would not use that terminology. You would not even be in that mindset. And we're in a time when young black boys and girls want to be pimps and strippers, because that is what they see. . . . Something is definitely wrong."

Lee says his grandmother, still alive at 99, saved all her social security cheques to put him through film school and he now feels blessed to be doing what he loves to do.

That stuff [in rap music videos] is not who we really are. We're more regal than that. We have more dignity than that, despite what is sold.

Sitting on a stool on the bare stage of Roy Thompson Hall, Lee held his audience rapt as he lit into what he called "gangsta rap craziness" that puts pimps on pedestals. He said parents today who let their children watch TV unsupervised, especially music videos, are guilty of a criminal act.

"That stuff is not who we really are. We're more regal than that. We have more dignity than that, despite what is sold."

Lee also stressed that while some black actors like Denzel Washington can now command $20 million a picture, they are still not in the positions of power in Hollywood that the so-called gatekeepers are, the people who decide what pictures get financed.

"I do believe that when we get in those positions, films like *Soul Plane* will not be made," he said to laughter and applause.

Soul Plane was a comedy about a black airline that served fried chicken and had Snoop Dogg as a pot-smoking pilot.

A Life of Dignity and Accomplishment

Lee said that when he was a kid growing up, he wasn't allowed to see Tarzan movies because of their insulting portrayal of Africans, and there was no Aunt Jemima syrup or Uncle Ben's rice products in their kitchen because of their demeaning stereotypes.

Lee was given a standing ovation at both the beginning and end of his monologue. At one point, the audience was thrilled when fellow filmmaker John Singleton, a Lee protege, joined him onstage.

Born Shelton Lee in pre–civil rights Atlanta, Ga. in 1957, the director moved at a very young age to Brooklyn, N.Y. His father was a Jazz musician and his mother an art teacher who nicknamed him Spike because of his tough nature.

His first film was issue-oriented—a 10-minute 1980 reworking of the classic but notoriously racist *Birth of a Nation*. Lee's major breakthrough came with 1986's sex comedy *She's Gotta Have It*. His landmark film was the race relations–themed *Do the Right Thing* in 1989.

Other notable titles include *Mo' Better Blues, Jungle Fever* and the biographical *Malcolm X*. He has become a notoriously outspoken show business personality, especially on issues of race in American society. But in 2003 he even indulged in legal action to try and stop the specialty channel Spike TV from infringing on his name. The issue was settled last year with the channel's owners, Viacom.

Violent Rap Lyrics Encourage Youth Violence

Brent Morrison

Brent Morrison is a newspaper columnist who writes about moral and ethical issues of national importance. His columns are featured in several California and Texas newspapers and on his Web site, http://brentmorrison.com.

It's not exactly stated, but a report issued by the American Psychological Association this month [May 2003] seems to conclude that words mean things.

I like to think so when I write anyway, though the study deals specifically with violent lyrics in songs. It's a subject worthy of consideration; the content of any CD that doesn't have a picture of [*Sesame Street* character] Elmo on it is suspect these days.

The average adolescent will argue that the words don't matter. They just like the beat, the rhythm, the guitar solos, the picture on the cover, the crinkle of the shrink-wrap, that new plastic smell, anything but the actual message. It's tempting to believe them given how many vocals are recorded in an angry mumble only eardrums under the age of 25 can understand, and that when you do catch a fragment you'll probably wish you hadn't.

The Effects of Violent Lyrics

In experiments on over 500 college students, who often work cheaper than guinea pigs and have less complicated musical tastes, subjects were found to experience an increase in aggressive thoughts after listening to songs with violent lyrics. Those

Brent Morrison, "Mean Music: Violent Lyrics and Aggression," *The Brent Morrison Column*, May 12, 2003. http://brentmorrison.com/Archives. Reproduced by permission.

subjected to the mean music were more apt to connect hostile meanings to words deemed to be violence neutral by the researchers.

It doesn't take a study to figure out that the constant pounding of nasty messages from music, television, movies, video games, and other amusements have a cumulative impact.

The words used in the study as "clearly aggressive" were blood, butcher, choke, fight, gun, hatchet, hurt, kill, knife, and wound. I understand that not everyone sees things the same way, but I worry about people who read hostility into inanimate objects like guns, hatchets, and knives. And to me, a butcher is the friendly old guy who had the shop at the end of the block when I was a kid, blood is the essence of life, and choked up is how I feel when I see a butterfly at sunrise.

OK, I got carried away, but you see the problem. The so-called "ambiguous" words are just as debatable: alley, animal, bottle, drugs, movie, night, police, red, rock, and stick. "Police" is probably as good a one-word Rorschach [interpretative] test [as] any but everyone knows that sticks and stones can break your bones. If you don't think "movie" is inherently violent you probably haven't wandered into a theater lately.

It Is the Words, Not the Music

Still, let's assume the choice of aggressive and neutral words was appropriate. The study found that the style of music had nothing to do with increased hostility. Thus "Mary Had a Little Lamb" performed by the hard rock band Korn would not increase aggression even though it wouldn't be confused for a lullaby. [Adult contemporary artist] Barry Manilow crooning rap lyrics might start a riot.

Aggression levels also went up after listening to humorous violent songs, which seemed like an oxymoron until I recalled the homicidal "Maxwell's Silver Hammer" by that noted death-rock ensemble, the Beatles. And what about Tom Jones [a singer considered sexy]? Good heavens, if he were a rap star every album he ever released would have a parental advisory warning.

Not that teens are flocking to buy the latest Tom Jones CDs. They probably don't like the beat. In any event if Jones' fifty-something female fans have ever torn up a Las Vegas nightclub I haven't heard of it.

Despite my quibbles with some of its points, the study's basic conclusion is right on the mark. Words do have meanings, meanings suggest thoughts, and thoughts lead to action. Most reasonably well-adjusted people will suffer no lasting harm from occasional exposure to violent content, but it doesn't take a study to figure out that the constant pounding of nasty messages from music, television, movies, video games, and other amusements have a cumulative impact.

It is said that we are what we eat; I'd argue that we become what we think. If so, perhaps we should pay as much attention to our entertainment diets as our waistlines.

CHAPTER 3

Is Rap Music Harmful to Women?

Chapter Preface

Surprising headlines began showing up in newspapers and magazines in 2007: "Sales of Rap Music Are Declining," "Hip-hop's Downbeat," and "Can Rap Regain Its Crown?" Statistics from several sources made it clear that the rap music industry was in trouble for the first time since its rise in popularity during the 1980s. According to the music trade magazine *Billboard*, sales of rap CDs dropped 44 percent since 2000. Although all music sales were down from 2006 according to Nielsen SoundScan, rap sales were down 33 percent, which was twice the amount for the music industry overall. Moreover, for the first time in twelve years, no rap album hit the top-ten list for bestsellers of the year. Eminem's album *The Eminem Show* became the hottest-selling album five years before, but no other album sold as well since that success. Formerly overshadowing all other music genres, rap sales trailed those for country and heavy metal music. The trend was so dramatic that rap artist Jay-Z cast himself as Superman trying to save hip-hop in his November 2006 CD *Kingdom Come*, and a month later artist Nas titled his album *Hip Hop Is Dead*.

What is causing the shrinking size of this music giant? Filmmaker Byron Hurt believes that rap music fans are getting tired of raunchy lyrics, including content that degrades women by depicting them as sex objects, whores, and conniving gold diggers. Hurt's PBS film *Beyond Beats and Rhymes* documents a growing critique of rap from within the culture itself. In previous years, burgeoning sales of albums deflated the protests of parents and other hip-hop outsiders who criticized the promotion of misogyny, drug use, and violence. This is a different matter, says Hurt, and the insider disillusionment is hitting promoters in their pockets.

So much so that the decline in sales is causing some in the industry to reconsider what goes into rap songs. Hip-hop mogul Russell Simmons recently developed the Hip-Hop Summit Action Network and recommended that artists and radio stations voluntarily bleep out offensive lyrics for broadcast. Owner of the multimillion-dollar No Limit Records, Master P, admits, "personally, I have profited millions of dollars through explicit rap lyrics." Understanding that he was once a part of the problem, he now wants to promote clean, positive music with his new label, Take A Stand Records. Similarly, musician KRS-One asserts, "The public has made a choice. They're saying, 'We do not want the nonsense that we see and hear on radio, and we are not putting our money there.' Rap music is being boycotted by the American public because of the images that we are putting forward."

It seems that the reason fans are passing up rap music, at least in part, is due to less tolerance for sexist representations of women. Tracy Denean Sharpley-Whiting, author of *Pimps Up, Ho's Down: Hip-Hop's Hold on Young Black Women*, certainly thinks so. As a young fan, she admits to being defensive in the face of hip-hop criticism, including that of the activist C. Dolores Tucker who crusaded against degrading rap lyrics in the 1990s. "Many of us weren't listening," says Sharpley-Whiting. "She was onto something," she continues, "but most of us said, 'They're not calling me a "bitch," they're not talking about me, they're talking about THOSE women.' But then it became clear that, you know what? Those women can be any women." Perhaps that is why a 2005 poll of black Americans by the Associated Press and AOL-Black Voices showed that half of the respondents believed rap was a negative force in American society. The authors of the following viewpoints express these and other views on the treatment of women in rap and hip-hop lyrics.

Rap Music Encourages Violence Against African American Women

Ewuare Osayande

Ewuare Osayande is an activist and author of several books including Misogyny and the Emcee: Sex, Race, and Hip Hop. *He is the creator of Project ONUS: Redefining Black Manhood, a series of antisexist workshops for black men.*

Hardly anyone in the Black community would advocate, support or sanction the rape and sexual assault of Black women; yet everyday Black women are being assaulted by Black male rappers, hip hop culture and the recording industry that condones, supports and profits from it.

From the lyrics on the radio to the videos on the tube, Black male rappers engage in an aural and visual assault on the minds and bodies of Black women. This cultural attack on Black women would warrant a state-of-emergency even if the madness began and ended in the studios, but it doesn't. More and more, Black men and boys are reciting these lyrics until they become the mental script that directs their interactions with Black women even as these tracks advocate the real-life hatred and violence toward women.

But what Nelly and his fellow rap cohorts fail to realize is that for every time they swipe a credit card through a Black female's behind and cash in on this oppressive profit-making scam, someone else is swiping one through their own asses as they remain bent in the position of submission to a system that views them as property too.

A Deadly Serious Problem

At face value, many would dismiss my description and assessment as being over the top, but upon close examination, one will realize that the critical condition of the situation cannot be overstated. My words fall way short of capturing the deadly effect misogynistic rap is having on Black women. The fact is that what many rappers are spewing is criminal by most societies' standards.

Clearly what rap has become, what it constitutes and perpetuates is a direct threat to Black women.

According to *Black's Law Dictionary* sexual assault is defined as "Any willful attempt or threat to inflict injury upon the person of another, when coupled with an apparent present ability so to do, and any intentional display of force such as would give the victim reason to fear or expect immediate bodily harm, constitutes an assault. An assault may be committed without actually . . . striking, or doing bodily harm, to the person of another."

As the definition clarifies, assault doesn't need actual physical contact to be considered such. The mere threat of violence is all that is required. Clearly what rap has become, what it constitutes and perpetuates is a direct threat to Black women who relate to men who listen to and are persuaded by a music that prides itself on being the epitome of reality, not the studio-contrived production that it really is. Given this, Black women walk under the constant threat of being preyed upon by men that step to the beat of a sampled drum loop produced by platinum-laced pied pipers who proclaim themselves pimps.

The combination of violent lyrics and pornographic images result in a poisonous concoction that is literally numbing our youth to the deadly ramifications of what the record industry has made rap to be. Increasingly rap is becoming synonymous with rape as record execs are using rap to violate the minds of our youth with pornographic images even as it works to justify and perpetuate the actual rape of Black women. . . .

Violence Against Women in Rap Music

It has become an expectation that every gangsta rapper's CD will have an obligatory "Beat that Ho" song in their rap repertoire. Gangsta rappers take the persona of the pimp as their street archetype of choice. To be a pimp means that the possibility of slapping, beating or otherwise assaulting a woman is just a look or a word away. This valorization of violence sits at the center of the current image of the rapper. And many rappers are being turned out by an industry that is invested in keeping Black men in the role of violent-prone sexual predator.

50 Cent, one of the most popular rappers on the scene today, is heard intimidating a woman on his 2003 top ten track, "P.I.M.P." that stayed in rotation on radio for weeks upon its release:

> Bitch choose with me, I'll have you stripping in the street/
>
> Put my other hoes down, you get your ass beat/
>
> Now Nick is my bottom bitch, she always come up with my bread/
>
> The last n---a she was with put stitches in her head.

Beanie Sigel's "Watch Your Bitches" from his Def Jam release entitled *The Reason* takes an even more morbid turn when he threatens a woman with

> bye bye bitch/
>
> f--- that red dress on/
>
> get a head step on/

speed on before you get peed on/

when I piss I don't miss/

get mad, scratch your ass and get glad/

before I scratch your ass and get Glad bags/

throw your shit out on the trash.

The celebrated rap producer Dr. Dre is heard in his rap "Housewife" from the CD *Dr. Dre 2001* saying,

Naw hoe is short for honey/

almost had her wailing like Bunny/

telling tales of being pregnant, catching Nordstrom sales with abortion money/

I spotted her seeing her with my n---as when I shot at her.

On Lil Jon's track "Bitches Aint Shit" from the popular *Crunk Juice* CD, he regurgitates the master/slave relationship with him, a Black man, assuming the role of the master with the Black woman as his slave.

Acting all sophisticated spending money that she didn't make/

I get so mad that I could slap her acting like she Cleopatra/

aint no need to ask she's a slave to the money and I'm the master.

Snoop Doggy Dogg has an entire track about beating women on his latest [2004] CD *R&G: (Rhythm and Gangsta) The Masterpiece*. The rap, "Can U Control Yo Hoe" has Snoop schooling another guy on how to beat the woman he is living with. The chorus is instructive in its brutality:

Can you control your hoe? (You got a bitch that won't obey what you say)/

You can't control your hoe? (She hardheaded, she just won't obey)/

Can you control your hoe (You've got to know what to do, what to say)/

You've got to put that bitch in her place, even if it's slapping her in her face/

Ya got to control your hoe/

Can you control your hoe?

These self-admitted womanizers and women-beaters are rewarded and celebrated in our society, and we see nothing wrong with this?

Later in the track he says,

What kind of pimp holds back?/

Never met a bitch that a pimp can't slap/

What's wrong with pimpin'?

This is the same Snopp Dogg that gets featured in movies and commercials selling fabric softener! It is also the same Snoop Dogg that produces porn and "Girls Gone Wild" videos. These self-admitted womanizers and women-beaters are rewarded and celebrated in our society, and we see nothing wrong with this?

From Words to Deeds?

Some might argue that this is just a case of "boys being boyz." "No harm done. They're just acting. It's all entertainment." But as an article in a recent issue of *Vibe* magazine delineates, this verbal assault is just a description of what many of these rappers actually do in their personal lives.

According to the article "Rap's Black Eye" rapper Big Pun (now deceased) sent his wife Liza Rios to the hospital three times over the course of their ten year relationship and "prevented her from seeking medical attention on many other occasions." Recounting one episode Liza Rios is quoted as saying, "One time he told me to change the batteries in his beeper. I totally forgot about it, and he took a lead pipe and started swinging on me. I had my daughter in my arms, and I told Cuban (another rapper) to take the baby. After he finished beating me, my elbow was twisted out of place. I was limping for two months." For Liza Rios and numerous other women, the last thing this is is entertaining.

As Elizabeth Mendez Berry questions expose the main issue here: "When you get paid to call every woman a ho, at what point do you start believing you are a pimp?" 50 Cent's rap, "P.I.M.P." would suggest as soon as the ink on your recording contract dries. And many rappers and would-be rappers are in agreement with him.

Rapper Mystical of "Shake that Ass" fame pleaded guilty to sexual battery after assaulting a woman in January 2004—an incident that was caught on video tape. Damon Dash has had at least one order of protection granted against him and has been arrested several times for reported domestic abuse. Busta Rhymes has also had a restraining order imposed against him by a woman who has children by him. Rapper Charli Baltimore has gone on record describing the abuse she experienced at the hands of none other than the Notorious B.I.G. (Christopher Wallace). Also, friends of his wife Faith Evans have spoken out about how the bruises she covered under make-up and sunglasses didn't stop until after his murder.

A childhood friend of Wallace has said that he "treated women like a pimp with his hos. He would talk about hitting them. He'd say things like, 'She was out of pocket, so I had to put that bitch back in line.'"

Once you start calling someone a dog, it is not a stretch to begin treating them like a dog.

Biggie protégé and former partner of Dash, Jay-Z, would find himself embroiled in a controversy after video of him smacking on a woman repeatedly surfaced on the net. His Roc-A-Fella Records, in L.A.P.D. [Los Angeles Police Department] fashion, would have us not believe our lying eyes and claim that the video tape was wrong. Their press statement titled, "Jay-Z Was Not Beating a Woman," is a clear attempt at damage control. They would have us believe that it was a case of Jay-Z just playing around with an old friend from the neighborhood. "Love taps. That's all. She was enjoying herself as she was being knocked to the floor!"

Dehumanizing Black Women

The Black community's relative reluctance to call this behavior for what it is—sexist—and resist it on all fronts as an act of sexual assault on all Black women, has resulted in the normalization and general acceptance of calling Black women by a name used to refer to a female dog. And once you start calling someone a dog, it is not a stretch to begin treating them like a dog.

Pearl Cleage details the socialization process that teaches us all to accept the dehumanization of Black women when she writes in *Mad at Miles* that,

> It is impossible to live in America and not be tainted by sexism and a participant in it, either as a victim or a perpetrator. As women, by the end of our African American girlhoods, we have learned and perfected a dizzying variety of slave behaviors which we are rewarded for mastering by the men who made them up in the first place.

As men, they were taught that we were inferior, unworthy of their respect, subject to their whim and present on earth primarily for their sexual pleasure and the bearing and mothering of their children.

We were all taught that it is acceptable for them to hit us when they think we have "asked for it" and that their opinions carry more weight in all critical decisions simply because they were men and therefore assumed to be of superior knowledge and more vast experience.

Taking Responsibility

No, rap music did not start the abuse, assault or rape of Black women, but it does advocate, glorify, justify and condone it— and as such—it works to reinforce and ensure its continuation and survival. Rap music and the rappers who create and produce it are responsible for the impact of their message on the minds of impressionable youth. When a sixteen or seventeen year old boy hears a rapper he admires counsel him to "smack that bitch," why do we think that he would not consider doing that? What other force is as compelling that is advising him not to strike a woman, when the majority of mediums in American life only reinforce his destructive desires? Who are we fooling? None but ourselves if we think we can deny the impact rap(e) music is having on the minds and behavior of our youth. These would-be men are living their lives saturated by a socially accepted soundtrack that is riddled through with references to women as dogs that can and should be treated as such, kicked or killed at will.

In her article, Elizabeth Mendez Berry cites the scary stat that "Murder at the hands of a romantic partner is a leading cause of [death] among African American women between the ages of 15–24 according to the National Center for Health Statistics. The bruised bodies of Black women in inner-city streets and suburban homes are proof enough of the damage being done in the name of being true to a game that nobody wins."

Smackfest

Further evidence of the normalization of abuse and assault of Black women is popular New York radio station Hot 97's "Smackfest." Promoted like a pro boxing match, two women are squared off in a contest to see who can outlast who as they take turns smacking each other in the face with the hope of winning a consolation prize. In one video contest one woman is slapped to the point of busting her lip. The Black male DJ stops the match intervening with "we got mouth blood," only to have them return and keep beating on each other.

Just when you thought the culture could not get any more crass, here comes Smackfest.

Smackfest has currently been shut down by New York state officials after City officials intervened, citing a state law that protects people from dangerous and demeaning competitions. According to the State Athletic Commission, Smackfest is an unlicensed and illegal boxing match that could lead to Hot 97 executives and their parent company Emmis Communications being indicted and charged.

Smackfest represents the latest stage in the devolution of hip hop culture. Just when you thought the culture could not get any more crass, here comes Smackfest. Now that the abuse of Black women has been normalized, embraced and defended, poor Black women are being super-exploited and their rights violated to increase radio ratings. A stew of hyper-sexual sadomasochistic rhetoric and imagery bombards the senses of America's youth everyday and Black females are the most targeted and hardest hit. And now many are being programmed to see no wrong in hitting each other. Rendered invisible as they are simply seen as hoes, bitches, nameless gold-diggers who will do just about any damn thing for a dollar even allow themselves to be peed, spat, or hit on for the hope of getting paid and being seen. . . .

Black Women Are Standing Up

But sisters ain't waiting on us brothers to get our act together. Although conditions are beyond dismal, Black women are not taking this lying down. Many women have been, and even more are becoming, active in their local communities. Black women all over this country are taking their bodies back from the marketplace, resisting violence and domestic abuse, redefining their relationships to men and this male dominant system.

Nationally, Aishah Simmons' *NO! The Rape Documentary* has become a rallying cry for our times. Her nearly decade-long sojourn to give voice to the silenced memories of Black female survivors of rape, incest and sexual molestation stands as a clear example that African American women are refusing to remain silent.

Let us . . . build up a new generation of Black men who refuse to define manhood based on their ability to manipulate, control or otherwise threaten the lives of women.

When rapper Nelly wanted to host a bone marrow drive on Spelman's [college] campus, Black women protested to hold him accountable for his demeaning display of Black women in his music and videos. Moya Bailey, president of the Feminist Majority Leadership Alliance, and other student activists had to withstand a barrage of criticism from every side—and did—in the effort to make their point. They were not about to allow Nelly to come to use them in his effort to make himself look good only to turn around and make another (s)exploitative video.

Conferences and community dialogues are taking place all over the country and many more are still needed. Not only is our future at stake, our very present is precarious. What we do now is what matters most.

Black Men Need to Stand Up, Too

As Black men, we are challenged and encouraged by none other than the man that [actor and social advocate] Ossie Davis called "our living Black manhood," [civil rights leader] Malcolm X. Let us be guided in this work by Malcolm's self-critical words as expressed in a letter written to his cousin-in-law Hakim Jamal just one month before his assassination as quoted in an essay written by Barbara Ransby and Tracye Matthews published in the anthology *Words of Fire*:

> I taught brothers not only to deal unintelligently with the devil or the White woman, but I also taught many brothers to spit acid at the sisters. They were kept in their places— you probably didn't notice this in action, but it is a fact. I taught these brothers to spit acid at the sisters. I taught the brothers that the sisters were standing in their way. I did these things brother. I must undo them.

Let us in the spirit of "Our Living Black Manhood" also undo the spitting of acid at the sisters that still continues and in so doing build up a new generation of Black men who refuse to define manhood based on their ability to manipulate, control or otherwise threaten the lives of women.

Until we do, how can we expect Black women to trust us?

[Writer] Pearl Cleage, speaking to women, gives us men direction on this question.

> If Black men won't admit that their sexism and male chauvinism and domestic violence are problems, how can we consider them allies in the search for creative solutions? We can't. Not yet. Not until they are willing to redefine their Black male reality to incorporate the equally valid reality of

our Black female experiences. Not until they are prepared to recognize their role as oppressors in the struggle against sexism and see their crimes as no less serious than the crimes committed in defense of racism.

Chicano Rap Is Hyper-Masculine and Misogynist

Pancho McFarland

Pancho McFarland is a professor of sociology at Chicago State University. He is the author of many articles about rap music and the book Chicano Rap: Gender and Violence in the Postindustrial Barrio.

Growing up in northern New Mexico my models of Chicano/Mexican American masculinity and femininity were varied. My grandfather and his brothers were gentle men who gained satisfaction from positive, mutually edifying human interaction with men and women. They taught me about compassion and love. My friends presented a tough, hyper-masculine facade they learned from their eastside barrio and from the violence they saw around them in the boxing gym, the streets and, importantly, in our mass media. They taught me how to fight.

My models of Chicana/*Mexicana* womanhood, the women in my family, did not take shit from anyone—including their husbands. They were strong and caring. Their endless stories emanating from the kitchen and the poker table taught me about the pitfalls of being a male chauvinist pig, while at the same time they warned my sister to be chaste and not get a "reputation."

The Influence of Rap

I began learning to be a "man" by dare-deviltry and drinking in the early 1980s, the same time that rap and hip hop culture began to break out of its original home in New York City and go nationwide. Rap images of black masculinity combined

Pancho McFarland, "Hyper-Masculine and Misogynist Violence in Chicano Rap," *Bad Subjects*, September 2002. http://bad.eserver.org. Reproduced by permission.

with those of Mexican American masculinity to inform my search for manhood. By the late 1980s I was firmly ensconced in academia and rap had burst onto the pop culture stage. In 1990 Kid Frost became the first Chicano to make it in the rap game. His *Hispanic Causing Panic* LP and hit single "La Raza" were godsends for me and other Chicano rappers and break-dancers. Unfortunately, its hyper-masculine bravado mirrored the attitudes that led me and many of my friends to fight, drink, consume drugs and otherwise harm ourselves and others.

My first question was why do these young men spend so much time thinking about, writing about, and listening to stories of violence?

Later, in the midst of writing my dissertation I used rap music as a way of confronting the academy's most racist and classist elements, and to re-affirm my identity as a brown man steeped in the traditions of working-class Hispano New Mexico. Rap's aggressive beats, cacophonous production styles and often-angry lyrics spoke to me as a Chicano in the Ivory Tower. They responded to the institutions that oppressed them, the police, the schools, etc., in ways that at times I wished I could have responded to the oppression I experienced at the university. I co-authored my first article on rap, "Quiet as It's Kept: Rap as a Model for Resisting the Academy," in 1998. Since then I have written several pieces focused on Chicano rap.

Cholo Rap

In the last four years the violence of Chicano rap has made a profound impression on me. Chicano rappers rap about hitting each other, hitting cops, and hitting and abusing women. My first question was why do these young men spend so much time thinking about, writing about, and listening to stories of violence? For me, rap and hip hop culture, had been about escaping violence and oppression. It was about getting together and expressing ourselves with our bodies and voices. Of course, break-dancing battles often turned violent and people fought at parties that showcased hip hop culture. Nonetheless, hip hop was mostly a safe space. So, why all the violence in Chicano rap today?

First, understanding Chicano rap requires examination of Mexican male expressive culture, black male expressive culture and the dominant culture. Second, our society is in the midst of a crisis of masculinity attracting men to consume and produce violent popular culture. Third, the extreme misogyny in Chicano rap results from our notions of masculinity that equate manhood with demeaning the Other, especially women.

Gangsta-style rap was a natural direction in which to take Chicano male expressive culture.

The first and most direct model of masculinity informing the narratives of Chicano rappers comes in the form of Mexican male oral culture and traditions. In my community the question about boxing was not whether to box or not, but when you would get into your first fight. We revered the Chicano lumpenproletariat [dispossessed individuals cut off from their own society], the *cholo* and *pachuco* who dished out more pain than he received. We drew pictures of the *cholo*, dressed like him, spoke like him, and behaved like him. Many of us became him. Why not? The cholo challenged his oppression with gun in hand. Girls liked him. He was strong, handsome and brown. We heard the *corridos* and other Mexican (American) music that celebrated the social bandit who protected himself and his people "with his pistol in his hand." We heard the stories of our distant relatives who rode with Poncho Villa fighting for land and liberty in the Mexican Revolution, and others who fought, died and killed for their country in World War II, Korea and Vietnam. The brave, honorable Mexican man fought. Violence and hyper-masculinity became somewhat of a norm for young Chicanos.

Mixtures of Masculinity

As a result of the commodification of blackness in the larger US culture through rap and the gangxploitation film genre, we had a new model of hyper-masculinity: the Bad N---a. In black male oral culture the Bad N---a has a long history similar to the male Mexican hero figure. From [rapper] Stagga Lee to [fictional private investigator] Shaft to [rapper] Ice-T, the Bad N---a served as a symbol of defiant black manhood. Since both black and Mexican male cultures lauded the strong, often violent man, we were familiar with the new postmodern social bandit, the black gangsta. Gangsta-style rap was a natural direction in which to take Chicano male expressive culture. It was aggressive, hyper-masculine and "real."

To be a man is to shun the feminine like a virus.

During the 1980s we also witnessed the rise of the Hollywood blockbuster movie that more often than not featured a violent male hero. He didn't allow anyone to get over on him; he, too, seemed to be loved by the women. We also became victims of the flood of guns and drugs into our communities, and the economic violence of the [U.S. president Ronald] Reagan years that led many to turn to illicit entrepreneurship as their means of survival. Economic restructuring led to extreme poverty in some communities, which according to the get-tough-on-crime logic could only be contained with more cops and more prisons. Gang task forces were created to keep young brown men in their neighborhoods and an all-out War on Youth of Color followed. Police have become militarized and now turn on us the high-tech weaponry and communication systems used to defeat foreign enemies.

The media helped disseminate the hateful War on Youth of Color by presenting us as the face of violence. News stories featuring brown and black men warned middle-class America about the gang menace. Sensationalized stories of innocent victims, usually white, being killed by drive-by shootings filled the airwaves. While the CIA [Central Intelligence Agency] and the US military quietly destroyed much of Central America, the media loudly declared the existence of an epidemic of minority youth violence. As a result few outside the *barrios* and ghettos questioned commando raids in the inner-city that destroyed homes and families, and criminalized and imprisoned a large part of an entire generation.

Hyper-Masculinity Through Shunning Femininity

So violence exploded in the *barrios*. It seeped into our homes through our TV screens and into our hoods through police and gang violence. With this legacy of violence in our expressive culture and our streets, one shouldn't be surprised at the hyper-violence narrated by Chicano rappers. Nonetheless, I can't stop asking why. Violence isn't the only occurrence in the *barrio*. We hate, but we also love. We go to church, dance, laugh, and care for our gardens. We hug our children, party with friends, and respect life. Yet none of this makes it onto rap CDs. Rappers leave out most of what occurs in our *barrios* and small towns, along with the social privilege that destroys us. Why?

Boys are taught hyper-masculinity from Day One. "Don't cry!," "Don't be a sissy!," "You throw like a girl!" shout our fathers and mothers, teachers and coaches. To be a man is to not be a woman. And a woman is weak, frail, and passive. To be a man is to shun the feminine like a virus. Signs of weakness are a "no-no." In our either-or dichotomous system of logic, weakness is the opposite of strength. A young man demonstrates his strength through daily performances of violent masculinity because, as [sociologist] Michael Kimmel points out, as soon as you have proven your manhood through acts of daring you must prove it again or risk the labels "pussy" or "fag." Moreover, the corporate media's violent, masculine superheroes—the [Sylvester] Stallones, [Bruce] Willises and [Arnold] Schwarzeneggers—dominate the pop culture landscape. These are our models of manhood.

So we run from the feminine. We dehumanize women with our jokes and locker-room lies. All the while violence against women increases, sanctioned by our popular culture. The slasher genre of Hollywood film and a large sector of commercial rap legitimize the victimization of women. In the end objectified female images dehumanize women and further entrench male privilege.

Discussing violence helps Chicanos better understand life and death and the struggle for humanity.

Consuming and Creating Violence

Still young men wouldn't focus their aesthetics almost entirely on violence if violence didn't sell. Young Chicanos trying to make it out of the *barrio* rap about violence because they have astutely analyzed the rap music marketplace and see that three central themes have cornered the rap industry. Sex, violence and money sell better than love, kindness and generosity. After the late 1980s when rap became a multi-billion dollar industry, themes related to politics, social criticism and alternative lifestyles fell by the wayside. Greed and violence fill the airwaves and young Chicanos listen to the radio. As [African American author and social activist] bell hooks argues, perhaps the question should not be why Chicano rappers focus on violence, but rather why we consume it. Our video games, films, televisions, and music normalize and naturalize violence. Instead of seeing violence as a social ill, it excites and entertains us. Violence sells and we consume it.

However, this doesn't mean that Chicano rappers are simply duped by a violent system into creating an aesthetic of violence. Violence isn't simply a picture on a screen or an image in a song. It is real and disproportionately affects poor, inner-city youth of color. While a great deal of violence is gratuitous and packaged as a commodity to be consumed as entertainment, Chicano rappers also attempt to analyze the very real violence around them. When Sir Dyno asks "What Have I Become?" as a result of a violent lifestyle or when the Latin Bomb Squad question the eye-for-an-eye mentality that kills homies and devastates families, they aren't simply glorifying violence or parroting our violent society.

This seemingly nihilistic obsession with violence is, as [anthropology and Latin studies professor Nicholas] De Genova argues, a means by which young Chicanos cope with the violence around them and examine questions about humanity. Discussing violence helps Chicanos better understand life and death and the struggle for humanity. In an environment saturated with economic and physical violence, Chicano rappers make meaning of our world through the contemplation of death.

A New Masculinity from an Old Masculinity

Where are Mexican men like my grandfather? Many still live in their communities. Why aren't their models of masculinity more prominent in popular culture? Why aren't their voices heard? Has globalized, homogenized mass culture replaced interpersonal relationships that we once relied on to structure our manhood and womanhood?

We must remember these men. But, perhaps more importantly, we should embrace positive aspects of femininity to counter the epidemic of hyper-masculinity. The violent, destructive rage of rappers should be challenged by a constructive rage informed by positive notions of womanhood, manhood and Mexican-ness. Chicano rap's violence should not be censored or shunned. Instead, we should engage these young men in an intra-cultural and intergenerational dialogue that takes into account the multiple perspectives and heterogeneous lives of women and the myriad ways of being Mexican men.

To combat the crippling violence and misogyny in our communities and youth we must educate ourselves and our children in the egalitarian, democratic, and communal aspects of our culture.

In an interview for the Voices of Freedom film project Bernice Johnson Reagon informs us that she constantly begs older black people to teach all that they know of black culture and traditions. She tells them "don't go to the grave with your knowledge."

Similarly, I challenge Mexican-origin elders to intervene in the hip hop community. Do not write off our children as hopeless. To combat the crippling violence and misogyny in our communities and youth we must educate ourselves and our children in the egalitarian, democratic, and communal aspects of our culture. We should study and discuss the work of writers like Ana Castillo and Cherrie Moraga, artists like Yolanda Lopez, and filmmakers like Esperanza Vasquez. Engaging rappers in a mutually respectful dialogue that uses the cultural production of Chicana feminists as a counterweight to cultural violence can open new ideas of masculinity and humanity, so sorely needed in this era.

Women and Men Need to Take a Stand Against Misogynist Rap

Jenee Osterheldt

Jenee Osterheldt is the lifestyle columnist for the Kansas City Star *newspaper in Missouri.*

In *Hustle & Flow*, this summer's [2005] critical movie darling, DJay, a pimp who wants to be a rapper, rhymes: "That's the way the game goes, gotta keep it strictly pimpin/Gotta have my hustle tight, makin' change off these women, yeah."

The sad thing is those lyrics are not only a pimp's reality. A lot of rappers, too, are making money by degrading women.

And for the first time in a long time, many women are getting fed up with these one-sided, shameful images of females in videos and songs.

Misogyny Is the Norm

There's a horde of songs shaming women stampeding the airwaves this summer [2005].

"Wait" by the Ying Yang Twins: The Twins think it's sexy to describe their organs and aggressive sexual prowess. Their current single, "Badd," describes their ideal woman, who will move like she has something to prove and is a schoolgirl by day and stripper by night.

"Give Me That," by Webbie, has the young rapper practically demanding sex from a female and demeaning her while he is doing it.

"Ass Like That," by Eminem, parodies hip-hop's saturation with sexually explicit lyrics.

And BET's late-night "Uncut" showcases soft-pornlike videos by Nelly, Ludacris, 50 Cent and other rappers.

"The misogyny has always been there," says Serena Kim, features editor for *Vibe* magazine.

It's becoming harder for women of the hip-hop generation to defend the culture when the mainstream is latching on to the ho-stomping, booty-shaking elements of hip-hop.

"But it's different now because the culture is bigger and mainstream. Now every kid in America is well versed in hip-hop."

Going Too Far?

It's becoming harder for women of the hip-hop generation to defend the culture when the mainstream is latching on to the ho-stomping, booty-shaking elements of hip-hop.

The tipping point for many people came last year [in 2004] via BET's "Uncut," when Nelly swiped a credit card down the backside of a stripper in his "Tip Drill" video.

Kim says that video and the lyrics crossed the line.

Spelman College, a historically black college for women in Atlanta, made headlines last year when it banned Nelly from performing at the school unless he engaged in a dialogue about "Tip Drill."

He declined.

Women Demand Change

From there, a snowball began to roll. Earlier this year [2005], *Essence* kicked off a "Take Back the Music" campaign to raise the level of dialogue on how women are depicted in popular culture. Throughout the year the magazine will run features that explore the hypersexuality in hip-hop, and each feature will include actions readers can take to help fight the negative imagery. Organizers say the goal is not to ban hip-hop music or enforce censorship but to bring attention to the imbalance.

"We aren't attacking hip-hop," says Cori Murray, arts and entertainment editor of *Essence.* "There are still very good things in hip-hop; I love hip-hop."

Misogyny in hip-hop, however, is running rampant, Murray says, and what's popular in hip-hop is misogynistic and headed toward porn.

"If we [black women] start telling them, 'Stop calling us that,' or, 'Stop showing us that way,' think about what could happen," she says. "We have so much power. I doubt these guys are going to turn their backs on us."

A Complex Problem

Joc Max, a well-known Kansas City party DJ and producer, says women aren't solely responsible for change.

"We have to take a stand as men and realize we have control, we can teach our youth and help our children. We can have a good time without singing songs like 'Wait' or [exploiting] scantily clad young women."

Rich Lester, Kansas City hip-hop producer known as Jkr70, says an answer is complicated.

I feel like I need a shower after [listening to] some of those records.

"It's like a company that has been run badly for so long that you have to get another job; that's the state of the music industry," he says. "The path should have been steered in a different direction a long time ago. Now it's about the money, and sex sells. It's just not my bag. I am a guy's guy, and I don't need to hear some of that stuff. It just makes me uncomfortable."

Joc Max decided to get a new bag when the music got too raunchy.

"There is no gray area—you roll with it or don't," he said. "But I choose to not play that music. I feel like I need a shower after [listening to] some of those records.

"I have to get deeper; I have to move on. Rap is part of hip-hop, and it came from funk, so I am going to play that. The awkward position for me is which venues are going to be risk-takers and allow me to play a different form of hip-hop. I might be less popular now, but at least I have my integrity."

When it comes to radio, Julee Jonez says as a radio personality, she's on the fence.

"We are put in a hard spot because we don't directly choose the music," says Jonez, co-host of "The Breakfast Jam" on KPRS-FM in Kansas City. "But we have to guard ourselves and use the most-clean versions possible. But we do receive backlash. If we pull every Lil Jon and Ying Yang Twins song off the air, the numbers will suffer."

Compelling Women to Comply

The "video vixen," recognized as a voluptuous, half-naked and often gyrating model in music videos, is another factor figuring into the rise of misogyny in the industry, Jonez says.

"It has gotten glorified by our younger ladies—and you have your people like Common who don't do that—but the majority of people in the club are listening to Ying Yang Twins and 'Tip Drill,'" she says.

If there is anyone who knows about the effects of video models, it's Karrine Steffans, author of "Confessions of a Video Vixen," a tell-all book about her hip-hop experiences.

Steffans has been in videos for Jay-Z, Mystikal, LL Cool J and R. Kelly and has been featured in magazines. She says video girls are on their own.

"I wish the industry would provide some sort of counseling. I wish someone would have told me what was going to happen or called me to see how I was doing. No one wonders how you are feeling or who you are."

As a model, "you are performing a service to help this man sell records," says Steffans, 26. "They give you the clothes to wear, tell you where to stand and how to move. If a man tells you to shake it like a salt shaker and you do it, [people reprimand you] and call you a ho."

The misogyny in music is a reflection of society, Steffans says, speaking from Los Angeles.

The answer [to misogyny in music] is women banding together.

"Society has changed when men aren't looking to protect women. There was a time when nobody would allow you to walk out of the house with tight shorts and a halter top, but now we are being exploited by our own men."

The answer, she says, is women banding together.

"We have to change our behavior," Steffans says. "We are the mother, the first teacher, and we, have to start our own revolution. We need to speak up and say we don't like this music, we don't want to wear these clothes, and we need to educate ourselves and stop letting the men get all that air-time."

Sexism Is Pervasive Throughout Culture

Edward Rhymes

Edward Rhymes has published numerous articles in critical race studies and black studies. He is also the author of When Racism Is Law & Prejudice Is Policy.

In this composition I will not be addressing the whole of hip-hop and rap, but rather hardcore and gangsta rap. It is my assertion that the mainstream media and political pundits—right and left—have painted rap and hip-hop with a very broad brush. Let me be perfectly clear, hardcore and gangsta rap is not listened to, watched, consumed or supported in my home and never has been. I will not be an apologist for anything that chooses to frame the dialogue about Black women (and women in general) and Black life in morally bankrupt language and reprehensible symbols.

In the wake of MSNBC's and CBS's firing of Don Imus [radio host who referred to a women's college basketball team in derogatory terms in 2007], the debate over misogyny, sexism and racism has now taken flight—or submerged, depending on your point of view. There are many, mostly white, people who believe that Imus was a fall guy and he is receiving blame and criticism for what many rap artists do continually in the lyrics and videos: debase and degrade Black women. A Black guest on an MSNBC news program even went as far as to say, "Where would a 66 year-old white guy even had heard the phrase nappy-headed ho"—alluding to hip-hop music's perceived powerful influence upon American culture and life (and apparently over the radio legend as well)—and

Edward Rhymes, "Caucasian Please! America's Cultural Double Standard for Misogyny and Racism," *Black Agenda Report*, April 18, 2007. Reproduced by permission.

by so doing gave a veneer of truth to the theory that rap music is the main culprit to be blamed for this contemporary brand of chauvinism.

Subculture or Mainstream?

However, I concur with bell hooks, the noted sociologist and black-feminist activist who said that

> to see gangsta rap as a reflection of dominant values in our culture rather than as an aberrant 'pathological' standpoint, does not mean that a rigorous feminist critique of the sexis[m] and misogyny expressed in this music is not needed. Without a doubt black males, young and old, must be held politically accountable for their sexism.

> Yet this critique must always be contextualized or we risk making it appear that the behavior this thinking supports and condones—rape, male violence against women, etc.—is a black male thing. And this is what is happening. Young black males are forced to take the 'heat' for encouraging, via their music, the hatred of and violence against women that is a central core of patriarchy.

There are those in the media, mostly white males (but also some black pundits as well), who now want the Black community to take a look at hip-hop music and correct the diabolical "double-standard" that dwells therein. Before a real conversation can be had, we have to blow-up the myths, expose the lies and cast a powerful and discerning light on the "real" double-standards and duplicity, Kim Deterline and Art Jones in their essay, "Fear of a Rap Planet," point out that "the issue with media coverage of rap is not whether African Americans engaged in a campaign against what they see as violent, sexist or racist imagery in rap should be heard—they should.... [W]hy are community voices fighting racism and sexism in mainstream news media, films and advertisements not treated similarly?

The answer may be found in white-owned corporate media's historical role as facilitator of racial scapegoating. Perhaps before advocating censorship of a music form with origins in a voiceless community, mainstream media pundits should look at the violence perpetuated by their own racism and sexism."

Scapegoating Rap

Just as the mainstream media and the dominant culture-at-large treats all things "Black" in America as the "other" or as some sort of science experiment in a test tube in an isolated and controlled environment, so hardcore rap is treated as if it occurred in some kind of cultural vacuum; untouched, un-bowed and uninformed by the larger, broader, dominant American culture. The conversation is always framed in the form of this question: "What is rap's influence on American society and culture?" Never do we ask, "What has been society's role in shaping and influencing hip-hop?"

The dominant culture's opposition lies with hip-hop's cultural variation of the made-in-the-USA misogynistic themes and with the Black voices communicating the message.

Gangsta and hardcore rap is the product of a society that has historically objectified and demeaned women, and commercialized sex. These dynamics are present in hip hop to the extent that they are present in society. The rapper who grew up in the inner-city watched the same sexist television programs, commercials and movies; had access to the same pornographic and misogynistic magazines and materials; and read the same textbooks that limited the presence and excluded the achievements of women (and people of color as well), as the All-American, Ivy-league bound, white kid in suburban America.

It is not sexism and misogyny that the dominant culture is opposed to (history and commercialism has proven that). The dominant culture's opposition lies with hip-hop's cultural variation of the made-in-the-USA misogynistic themes and with the Black voices communicating the message. The debate and the dialogue must be understood in this context.

Duplicitous Sexism and Violence in Black and White

In a piece I penned a couple of years ago, I endeavored to point out the clear ethnic and racial double-standards of the media and society as it pertains to sex and violence. My assertion was, and remains to be, that the mainstream media and society-at-large, appear to have not so much of a problem with the glorification of sex and violence, but rather with who is doing the glorifying. In it I stated that "if the brutality and violence in gangsta rap was truly the real issue, then shouldn't a [Mafia-themed] series like *The Sopranos* be held to the same standard? If we are so concerned about bloodshed, then how did [Mafia-themed] movies like 'The Godfather,' 'The Untouchables' and 'Goodfellas' become classics?"

I then addressed the sexual aspect of this double-standard by pointing out that "Sex & The City," a series that focused, by and large, on the sexual relationships of four white women, was hailed as a powerful demonstration of female camaraderie and empowerment.

This show, during its run, was lavished with critical praise and commercial success while hip-hop and rap artists are attacked by the morality police for their depiction of sex in their lyrics and videos. The don't-blink-or-you'll-miss-it appearance of Janet Jackson's right bosom during [a] Super Bowl halftime show . . . caused more of a furor than the countless commercials that (also aired during the Super Bowl) used sex to sell anything from beer to cars to gum. Not to mention the constant stream of commercials that rather openly talks about erectile dysfunction medication.

White Violence, Drugs, and Sex

The exaltation of drugs, misogyny and violence in music lyrics has a history that predates NWA [Niggaz with Attitude], Ice Cube, Ice T and Snoop Dogg. Elton John's 1977 song "Tickin," was about a young man who goes into a bar and kills 14 people; Bruce Springsteen's "Nebraska," featured a couple on a shooting spree, and his "Johnny 99," was about a gun-waving laid-off worker; and Stephen Sondheim's score for "Assassins," which presented songs mostly in the first person about would-be and successful presidential assassins.

Marilyn Manson declared that one of the aims of his provocative persona was to see how much it would take to get the moralists as mad at white artists as they got about 2LiveCrew.

Eric Clapton's "Cocaine" and the Beatles' "Lucy in the Sky with Diamonds" (LSD) as well as almost anything by Jefferson Airplane or Spaceship. Several songs from "Tommy" and Pink Floyd's "The Wall" are well known drug songs. "Catholic girls," "Centerfold," "Sugar Walls" by Van Halen were raunchy, misogynistic, lust-driven rock refrains.

Even the country music legend Kenny Rogers in his legendary ballad, "Coward Of The County," spoke of a violent gang-rape and then a triple-homicide by the song's hero to avenge his assaulted lover. Marilyn Manson declared that one of the aims of his provocative persona was to see how much it would take to get the moralists as mad at white artists as they got about 2LiveCrew. He said it took fake boobs, Satanism, simulated sex on stage, death and angst along with semi-explicit lyrics, to get the same screaming the 2LiveCrew got for one song. Manson thought this reaction was hypocritical and hilarious. . . .

Censoring Rap Will Not End the Problem

There have been many who have said that even with Imus gone from the airwaves, the American public in general and the Black community in particular will still be inundated by the countless rap lyrics using derogatory and sexist language, as well as the endless videos displaying women in various stages of undress—and this is true.

However, by that same logic, if we were to rid the record stores, the clubs and the iPods of all misogynistic hip-hop, we would still have amongst us the corporately-controlled and predominantly white-owned entities of Playboy, Penthouse, Hustler and Hooters. We would still have the reality TV shows, whose casts are overwhelmingly white, reveling in excessive intoxication and suspect sexual mores.

If misogynistic hip-hop was erased from American life and memory today, tomorrow my e-mail box and the e-mail boxes of millions of others would still be barraged with links to tens of thousands of adult entertainment web sites. We would still have at our fingertips, courtesy of cable and satellite television, porn-on-demand. We would still be awash in a society and culture that rewards promiscuity and sexual explicitness with fame, fortune and celebrity (reference Anna Nicole, Paris Hilton, Britney Spears).

And most hypocritically, if we were to purge the sexist and lewd lyrics from hip-hop, there would still be a multitude of primarily white bands and principally-white musical genres generating song after song glorifying sexism, misogyny, violence and lionizing male sexuality and sexual conquest.

Women Can Be Empowered by Rap Music

Layli Phillips, Kerri Reddick-Morgan, and Dionne Patricia Stephens

Layli Phillips is a professor in the Women's Studies Institute at Georgia State University in Atlanta. Kerri Reddick-Morgan is a graduate student in the Women's Studies Institute at Georgia State University in Atlanta. Dionne Patricia Stephens is a professor in psychology at Florida International University in Miami.

Women have been integral to the evolution of Hip Hop culture, especially rap music, since the beginning. Yet, historical accounts and critical analyses of the Hip Hop phenomenon have tended to downplay the contributions of women. Women have played pivotal roles as artists, writers, performers, producers, and industry executives. Women have influenced rap style and technique, ultimately shaping aesthetic standards and technological practices utilized by both women and men. Nevertheless, certain facts remain undeniable. First, men have outnumbered women in both the artistic arena and the corporate end of Hip Hop. Male rappers have outnumbered female rappers and male industry leaders have outnumbered female industry operatives. The production pipeline, from writers and performers to producers and executives, has effectively functioned like a modified "old boys' club," hampering women's entry and ascent to power within the industry in ways both subtle and overt. Now that Hip Hop has expanded beyond music into video production, clothing design, and other lifestyle enhancement domains, the processes impeding women's participation and power-sharing have only become more widespread.

Layli Phillips, Kerri Reddick-Morgan, and Dionne Patricia Stephens, "Oppositional Consciousness Within and Oppositional Realm: The Case of Feminism and Womanism in Rap and Hip Hop, 1976–2004," *Journal of African American History*, vol. 90, no. 3, summer 2005, pp. 254–260. Copyright © 2005 Association for the Study of African Life & History. Reproduced by permission.

Second, a masculinist discursive strand is clearly identifiable in both rap music and its parent culture, Hip Hop. The numerical preponderance of men, combined with pre-existing masculinist scripts [plans of action] and sexist practices in virtually all occupational and commercial realms as well as the society at large, has ensured the greater visibility of men's prerogatives and perspectives relative to women's in both rap music and Hip Hop. Due largely to masculinist biases already in place in the domains of advertising and news reporting, the public face of both Hip Hop and rap is masculine and the mainstream discourse of rap as Hip Hop's mouthpiece is masculine.

Hip Hop culture in general and rap music in particular provide a platform for African American women at street level to process and produce feminist and womanist ideas.

Challenging Assumptions

Third, both women and men have participated in Hip Hop culture and rap music in ways that have been both oppressive and liberatory [freeing] for women. To assume that men's voice or influence in Hip Hop or rap music has been uniformly sexist and that women's has uniformly opposed this sexism is to accept a false dichotomy that misrepresents the complexity of Hip Hop and rap with respect to gender. Furthermore, to assume that women have been the only feminist voices or influences within Hip Hop and rap is to negate the contributions of progressive, anti-sexist men within the movement. To claim that rap music and Hip Hop culture are purely and simply misogynistic is to view rap and the Hip Hop realm uncritically from the perspective of an outsider. In sum, Hip Hop, including rap music, is a complex and contradictory arena in which regressive and oppressive elements sometimes complicate and at times even undermine what fundamentally remains an oppositional and potentially liberatory project. . . .

Women in rap have maintained a dually oppositional stance within Hip Hop culture. On the one hand, this stance has allowed African American and Latino women to critique the sexism of men of their same race or ethnicity, using Hip Hop as a platform. On the other hand, this stance has enabled African American and Latino women to express solidarity with men of their same race or ethnicity in their critique of and struggle against mainstream society's racism, classism, and race-d sexism (which affects both women and men of color). One feature of the second aspect of women's oppositional stance in Hip Hop is that it has allowed "everyday" women of color to critique and contest certain aspects of . . . mainstream (including academic) feminism.

Feminism and Womanism in the Street

Popular music, as the folk music of the modern and postmodern eras, articulates the stories, philosophies, and yearnings of the masses. Hip Hop, encompassing one form of popular music (rap) and the culture that surrounds it, presents feminism and womanism at ground level or "the street." In the case of Hip Hop, "the street" is a site where the sensibilities of black lower class people prevail. Rap and Hip Hop artists come from and speak to a population that is not defined in terms of its academic credentials. While many rap and Hip Hop artists, like many members of their audience, are well educated and have college degrees, the erasure of distinctions related to educational attainment is generally valued over the emphasis on such distinctions. "Street knowledge" and "street smarts" are valued over formal education because of the history of African Americans' exclusion from formal education as a result of centuries of enslavement, colonization, legal segregation, and other forms of oppression and discrimination across the African diaspora [scattering of a people away from their ancestral homeland]. Street knowledge and street smarts are also valued because they facilitate the negotiation of postmodern living conditions. . . .

In terms of feminism and womanism specifically, Hip Hop culture in general and rap music in particular provide a platform for African American women at street level to process and produce feminist and womanist [feminism focused on the concerns of black women] ideas. Whether or not they endorse the labels "feminist" or "womanist" for themselves, women in Hip Hop are exposed to feminist and womanist ideas circulating within the general culture. Like other women, female hip hoppers discuss, adapt, translate, and sometimes even reject these ideas. One purpose of women's rap is to educate women and to motivate or inspire women to succeed in the face of problems they are likely to encounter in their lives. In rap, women speak to each other about various kinds of everyday occurrences as well as about recurring issues in the larger sociopolitical domain. In this realm, women support each other, critique each other, conscientize [persuade and rally] each other, challenge each other, and bear witness to each other. Another purpose of women's rap is to air women's concerns to men and provide a forum for discussion. Because gender is an accepted divide within the African American community, the discursive space created by women for women in rap is in many respects inviolate, even when women are using that space to communicate to or with men. Thus, while men may disagree with or reject what women rappers say, they generally engage them and respect women's right to utilize that platform.

Some Rap Music Is Respectful of Women

Lornet Turnbull

Lornet Turnbull is a reporter for the Seattle Times.

The images and lyrics are everywhere—on the radio, in music videos and in the boom emanating from car stereos on the streets.

They hype violence and denigrate women and enjoy a huge following, particularly among the hip-hip crowd.

A local [Seattle] social-service organization believes that such pop-culture messages breed aggression and may be contributing to an atmosphere that encourages sexual assaults against young women.

Armed with a $35,000 grant from the state, Southeast Youth and Family Services has teamed up with Seaspot Music Group for a yearlong campaign called "Respect Yourself: No Means No" aimed at young people.

Cleaning Up Rap Music

Seaspot, a promotions company that bills itself as the gateway to Seattle urban culture, will distribute free CDs with "clean" music aimed at countering the message of violent, gangsta rap. The CDs will be given away early next year [2006] to young people at parties, ballgames and shopping malls.

"We're trying to get a message to kids about respecting themselves and how that ties into this subculture of sexualizing everything that can lead young people into situations where they lose control," said Jeri White, executive director of Southeast Youth and Family Services.

At issue are gangsta-rap lyrics by such artists as 50 Cent and Dr. Dre that refer to women in derogatory terms or hip-hop videos that drip with violence and depict half-dressed young women in sexually explicit scenes.

Just because you see something on TV or hear something does not necessarily make it right. There'll always be dirt in the water; it's about giving young people a filter.

Seaspot's CEO [chief executive officer] Chukundi Salisbury, himself a DJ who sometimes plays these lyrics at parties and special events, said history is littered with failed attempts to take down gangsta rap. "We don't have the resources to fight the music industry," he said. "We're not anti-50 Cent because next year there'll be a different 50 Cent—a 75 Cent," he said. Acknowledging that he grew up listening to gangsta rap and still enjoys some of it, Salisbury said young people have become generally desensitized to this pop culture.

Cultivating an Atmosphere of Respect

"We're attacking the attitude; just because you see something on TV or hear something does not necessarily make it right. There'll always be dirt in the water; it's about giving young people a filter."

While there are no local statistics directly linking violent music and video images to sexual assaults, experts say such entertainment nonetheless creates an atmosphere that encourages them.

Mary Ellen Stone, executive director of the King County [Washington] Sexual Assault Resource Center said, "A lot of pop-culture messages reinforce sexual assault as acceptable."

Surveys of high-school students have shown, for example, that many believe if a guy takes a girl out and spends money on her, he has a right to expect something more.

"Challenging that kind of thinking is very important," she said.

Southeast Youth and Family will provide counseling services to victims of sexual assault as part of the campaign, which is being funded by a grant from the Washington Office of Crime Victim Advocacy.

CHAPTER 4

Does Rap Culture Perpetuate Violence?

Overview: The Complex Debate About Violence and Rap Culture

Michael Eric Dyson, John McCain, John Kerry, and Hilary Rosen

Michael Eric Dyson is a professor of theology at Georgetown University and the author of numerous books, including Holler if You Hear Me: Searching for Tupac Shakur. *John McCain is a U.S. senator and 2008 Republican presidential candidate. John Kerry is a Democratic U.S. senator who ran for president in 2004. Hilary Rosen is the former chairwoman and chief executive of the Recording Industry Association of America (RIAA) from 1993 to 2003.*

M*ichael Eric Dyson:* I think that what we've heard today is very compelling in terms of the necessity for an equally shared responsibility about the violence of American society, and how that violence is packaged, shaped, redistributed on the open market. And the marketing of violence, the seductions of violence, the titillations that are associated with violence, the erotic sheen that often accompanies violence, is something that is deeply problematic to many of us who are parents—like I am of three children—who are concerned about shaping the egos, shaping the mind-set, shaping the perspectives of young people in order to deter them from a life that is fruitless and to redirect them into paths and channels that are very productive.

Do Not Silence Young People

But the problem I have with so much of the discourse surrounding this issue of violence is that, implicitly, there is a function of censorship. We know that there is no explicit censorship. We know that all of us share in common the development of responses that defend the First Amendment. But there's an implicit censorship that goes on when we begin to give the voice and microphone to some groups of people and not to others. So what I'm concerned about—I'll make three very quick points and end here—what I'm concerned about is the necessity to hear from those young voices, those very powerful voices, sometimes admittedly angry voices, sometimes bitter voices, sometimes voices that are dipped into the deep pools of profanity, sometimes vulgarity. But I'm not so much concerned about the curse words, as the cursed worlds they occupy, and what hurt they experience in order to produce some of the deeply reflective, deeply self-critical, and also deeply problematic lyrics that they put forth.

So I think first of all, what's important about hearing from those young people—a disproportionate number of whom, by the way, happen to be African American and Latino voices—is that they tell truths about their situations that are avoided in textbooks and schools, and we dare say, in the United States Senate at some points, and synagogues and so on. The reality is that the violence is old and it has been around a long time. But the reality also is that we haven't really attacked certain forms of violence as equally as we have others. So that "The Duke" [actor] John Wayne would not be brought before a Senate committee to give a mea culpa for the way in which he romanticized and idealized this kind of western machismo that, dare we say, has informed even the Senate careers of some of our colleagues here today. But at the same time, Snoop Doggy Dogg is brought front and center, rhetorically and symbolically, if not literally, to talk about why it is that he chooses to make a living by telling the truth about what he understands. So violence in John Wayne [the star of movie Westerns] is acceptable. Violence in Snoop Doggy Dogg is not acceptable.

Which Violence Matters?

Number two, violence matters most when it occurs in the mainstream and not so-called outside of the mainstream. This is why we applaud President [Bill] Clinton for having the FTC [Federal Trade Commission] put forth this report after Columbine [the April 1999 Colorado high school shooting in which fifteen died and twenty-three were wounded]. But the reality is violence pervaded America way before Columbine. It struck Latino and African American communities in disproportionate numbers. And yet the rapper L. L. Cool J. by no means a hardcore rapper, released an album yesterday [September 12, 2000] that contained these lyrics, "I don't mean this in a disrespectful way / but Columbine happens in the ghetto every day / But when the crap goes down / y'all ain't got nothing to say." Now this is from a person who is well-received as an actor and as an entertainer in American society, but he understands that there has been a targeting—with vicious specificity—of African American and Latino communities when it comes to violence.

Those forms of violence are seen to be much more pathological and naturalized in a way that is destructive. And the violence of the larger society is not taken seriously until that violence happens in a mainstream white community where now it becomes a national problem, and a public health problem, and a plague. And we have to ask why is it that these voices that have been locked out, that have been marginalized, are seen [by their peers] as a necessity to articulate their understanding of the world, and sometimes violently so, to make a very powerful point?

Youth-Positive Legislation and Reform

Number three, if we're really concerned about the lives of kids, then we've got to not shred the safety net in terms of welfare reform, [because it] targets poor black and Latino and poor white kids in very specific ways. Because if there's diminished capacity for providing health care, and providing child care, for your children, that is much more destructive than a rap lyric that may or may not lead to a violent behavior. Also, we have got to stop this war on drugs that really has translated, as [African American civil rights leader and scholar] Lani Guinier said, into a war on black and Latino youth. And as you know, Mr. [John] McCain, the reality is that a report was issued earlier this year [2000] that the human rights of many African American and Latino youth are being violated. A report from Amnesty International was released saying that the American government ought to be ashamed of itself for the way in which it has stigmatized black and Latino youth in disproportionate fashion, leading to their arrest and their imprisonment, and therefore stigmatizing their lives for the duration of their time in this nation.

Furthermore, I heard this morning about the Senator expressing outrage about the video game that deals with the electrocution of a human being. And as repulsive as that is, the reality is, is that in Texas one hundred thirty some odd people have been legally executed on capital punishment for a capital crime. And a disproportionate number of those people happen to be black and Latino men. So I don't want to get rid of a game that may push our buttons in very problematic and provocative ways until we get rid of the very practices themselves that the game points to.

Finally, I think that—

John McCain: Mr. Dyson, I would agree with you if we still held public executions.

Dyson: Well, it's not about public executions. It's about if we do them in private, Senator McCain. The horrible shame that is going on in private is not publicly talked about. The horrible shame is not simply the exposure of the execution, it's the numbers of black and Latino men who are being subjected to this form of, I think, racially motivated legal lynching. So I think that, you're absolutely right in terms of the publicity, but the reality is that it's more shameful that it's not made more public so that more people can be outraged by it. Two more points—thank you so much for your indulgence.

Confronting Hidden Injustice

Another reason these young people have to be heard from—and we ought to hear their voices—is that they bear witness to the invisible suffering of the masses. And this is what I mean about publicity. We have to hear what they're talking about. We have to be confronted with what they're talking about even if we find it personally repulsive and reprehensible. So that for me, stigmatizing blacks, and avoiding the collective responsibility for the drug war, is something that needs to be talked about. Master P said, "I don't own no plane / I don't own no boat / I don't ship no dope from coast to coast." So we know that the flooding of black and Latino communities—whether intentionally or not, inadvertently or not—with drugs is not talked about as deeply and systematically as it needs to be. And yet the stigmatization of those who abuse drugs, who happen to be nonviolent offenders who end up in jail, needs to be talked about as well. And it's talked about much in rap music.

We need to hear those voices [of people of color] because many of these young people are disaffected from the political process.

Finally, in terms of racial profiling, the late rapper Tupac Shakur said, "Just the other day I got lynched by some crooked cops / and to this day those same cops on the beat getting major pay / But when I get my check, they taking tax out / so we paying the cops to knock the blacks out." Now here's a problem for commerce: the subsidization of your own oppression through tax dollars that lead to the imprisonment of your own people. That is something that needs to be talked about, and [often wouldn't be] were it not for these R-rated lyrics—that yes, contain repulsive narratives about rape, murderous fantasies that really are deeply destructive. But what's even more destructive is the environment in which they operate, the world in which they exist, and the world that curses them in a very serious and systematic fashion.

Representation for Youth of Color

I'll end here. We need to hear those voices because as [record producer and civil liberties activist] Mr. [Danny] Goldberg said ... many of these young people are disaffected from the political process. And one of the reasons they're disaffected from the political process—we can look here today. They're not being represented. With all due respect to the ingenuity of the Senate, for the most part, [Japanese American senator] Mr. [Daniel] Inouye and others are exceptions, this is a white male club. And if those people felt that they could have their own viewpoints, perspectives, and sensitivities respected in a profound way and [with] a kind of empathy that says that the person sitting across the board from me is really concerned about me because he or she has been through what I've been through, and therefore they know the circumstances under which I've existed, then we would have much more faith in the political process, that [it] would at least alleviate some of the suffering and the pain.

So for me, the reality is this: many of these young hip-hoppers certainly need to be talked to, and talked about, but more importantly, we should listen to them. Because the messages that they often put in our faces—that we don't want to hear because they make us uncomfortable—are the messages that we need to hear. The political process can only be enhanced; the American democratic project can only be strengthened; and the citizenship of America can only be deepened, with a profound engagement with some of the most serious problems that these young people represent—and tell us about. This is why—and I'll end here—Nas, a young rapper, said: "It's only right that I was born to use mics / And the stuff that I write is even tougher than dice." Absolutely true, and the reason it's tougher than dice—because they're rolling their dice in a world where they're taking a gamble that their voices can be heard, that their viewpoints can be respected, and that their lives can be protected.

Thank you very kindly, Senator. . . .

There is a particularly onerous aspect to the anger that is expressed in some of the lyrics. It's a kind of anger of domination that is particularly violent against women.

John Kerry: Mr. Chairman, thank you very much. It's been very interesting listening to a lot of this. I apologize that some of us have not been able to be here throughout it. I mean, as I said earlier today, there are some really tricky aspects to this that I know Senator Inouye was particularly sensitive to, and others I think have been. And Mr. Dyson, I was particularly struck—I came in—I didn't hear all of your testimony, but I couldn't agree with you more strongly about the perceptions of young people, and the difficulties of our trying to pass judgment on some aspects of what we hear. Certainly one person's profanity can easily be another person's protest. And that's always been true; it has always been true. And I can remember during the turmoil of the 1960s and early '70s in this country, there was an awful lot of profanity that was part of the political protest. And obviously, it would be sanctioned by the court under the First Amendment. And if I were black or Latino, or some other minorities in America, I could find a lot of four-letter words, and a lot of other kinds of words of powerful alliteration, with which to describe this institution and the political system's lack of response. I mean, after all, 48 percent of the kids in New York City don't graduate from high school.

Dyson: Right, right.

Kerry: There are more African Americans in prison today than in college.

Dyson: Yes.

Kerry: And if I were a young black person growing up in those circumstances in this country, notwithstanding the extraordinary opportunities that there are—and there are, I mean, just amazing opportunities for people. When you look at a person like Deval Patrick in Massachusetts, who came out of the South Side of Chicago, happened to get a great scholarship, went to Harvard, became the assistant attorney general for civil rights. I mean, there are people of enormous distinction who have made it. But the problem is, systemically, there is a sense, still, of much too great a set of hurdles and barriers. You look at what was in the paper, I think it was yesterday or today [September 12 or 13, 2000], that the reports are now—the surveys they're doing on the application of the death penalty—that is showing the same kinds of very disturbing trend lines with respect to race and otherwise. So I would caution my colleagues a little bit with respect to sort of a blanket statement with respect to what we hear. Music has always been a form of expression from the beginning of time, and an enormous political tool I might add. And in many cases it is.

The Problem of Violence Against Women

Now that said, it is really hard to find any excuse, and certainly any political redemption, in some of the lyrics that we see. There is, in fact, a particularly onerous aspect to the anger that is expressed in some of the lyrics. It's a kind of anger of domination that is particularly violent against women. And I am a parent, though my kids have now made it through college and seem to be okay, but I had serious reservations about that. And I think any parent has to have serious reservations about what they hear. My question to any of the panelists who could answer this adequately—and then I want to ask [president of the Motion Picture Association of America] Mr. [Jack] Valenti something about the movies per se. And of course there's a distinction between some of the music, between the software, between the video games, between the movies. There's a lot of gradation here, and we have to also be thoughtful about that.

But with respect to the music, it does strike me that some of what we've heard in the last ten years goes over a line that any responsible corporate entity ought to have second thoughts about sponsoring, notwithstanding some desire in the public at large to perhaps buy it. I can understand maybe pirate companies selling it. I could understand an underground network that makes some of it available. I find it very hard to understand why the most upright, upstanding, respected corporate entities in the country are advertising it, or on it, supporting it, investing in it. And I wonder if it—I mean, isn't there some measure, short of legislation and overreach by a legislative body—isn't there some way for a more adequate and responsible level of restraint to be exercised from the industry itself? Or is that simply, after all these years, asking too much?

Dyson: Can I add very briefly, in regard to that point, Senator Kerry? I think that—take, for example, what Ms. [Hilary] Rosen is saying. Take for example the first album by Notorious B.I.G., Biggie Smalls [*Ready to Die.* Now on that album, you would find stuff, I would find stuff, all of us, most of us, would find stuff that's pretty repulsive. His song celebrating his girlfriend is called "Me and My B----," and we can fill in the blanks there, even though he means it as a term of affection, and he goes on to iterate how this woman has really helped him and so on and so forth.

Censoring All Rap Doesn't Help the Problem

On that same album, he's got many other songs like "Things Done Changed": "Back in the days, our parents used to take care of us / Look at them now, they're even f------ scared of us / Calling the state for help because they can't maintain / Darned things done change / If I wasn't in the rap game, I'd probably have a ki [a kilo] knee-deep in the crack game / Because the streets is a short stop, either you're slinging crack rock or you got a wicked jump shot / Damn it's hard bein' young from the slums eating five cent gums / not knowing where your meal's coming from / What happened to the summertime cookout? Every time I turn around, a brother's being took out."

Now if you restrict, because of vulgarity, and profanity, and misogyny, and unwarranted sexism, the commercial viability of a particular album, on that same album is an eloquent exhortation for people to deal with.

Kerry: But that's not what I'm talking about.

People know when they are reading a lyric or a paragraph that has absolutely no value except the shock value.

Dyson: And I'm saying on the same album, though, the complex amalgam of the good and the bad company together.

Kerry: Sure, but that's not what I'm talking about. That's a powerful statement. I mean, at easy blush someone would say there's a—I mean, there's a whole lot contained in that. I don't think that's what I'm talking about. But I don't want to get bogged down here. I think most people—it's exactly what Jack Valenti said. You know, you can't necessarily define pornography, but you know when you see it. People know when they are reading a lyric or a paragraph that has absolutely no value except the shock value. And I think people can do that pretty well. And somehow that stuff finds its way into mainstream marketing. And I think you have to recognize this, and we all know how celebrity works in America, and we know how the marketing and sort of buildup is—you can create a demand for it, and you can create a sense of acceptability to it and build it into something more than any sort of real movement has created. So again, I don't want to get into this business.

Violence Sells

Hilary Rosen: That's not really true, with all due respect. You can't buy popularity. I mean, artists get popular because people are attracted to what they say. If you could buy popularity, 85 percent of the records that we put into the marketplace wouldn't fail.

Rap Musicians Associated with Violence Should Be Banned

Associated Press

The Associated Press is a not-for-profit cooperative that supplies news from around the world to newspapers, radio, television, and Internet platforms.

The Rev. Al Sharpton is putting in his two cents about the latest drama involving 50 Cent.

The civil rights leader on Tuesday [March 8, 2005] proposed a ban that would muzzle artists who are connected to any violent acts, denying them airplay on radio and television for 90 days. Though he did not single out 50 Cent by name, he told The Associated Press that a recent shooting linked to a feud involving 50 demonstrated the need for such a policy.

"There's a difference in having the right to express yourself and in engaging in violence and using the violence to hype record sales, and then polluting young Americans that this is the key to success, by gunslinging and shooting," he said.

Whether or not that's been the key to 50's success, he's certainly having a lot of it these days [2005].

Violence Involving Rappers

50 Cent is poised to debut at No. 1 on next week's [mid-March 2005] album charts with his new album, "The Massacre." The follow-up to his 2003 debut, "Get Rich or Die Tryin"—which sold 8 million copies—"The Massacre" is on track to sell about 1 million copies in just four days. In addition, he's got the nation's No. 1 single with "Candy Shop."

It comes a week after a bitter feud broke out involving the rapper and his former protege, The Game. A member of The Game's crew was wounded during a shooting outside a New York hip-hop radio station, where 50 Cent—who produced part of The Game's platinum-selling debut album—was on the air, announcing that he was kicking him out of his G-Unit clique.

No one has been arrested for the shooting, and police are still investigating the incident, but some in the media have suggested it may have been the beginning of a violent dispute between the two rappers, who flaunt a gangsta image: Both are former drug dealers and both have been shot multiple times. There have been comparisons to the feud between Tupac Shakur and the Notorious B.I.G. nearly a decade ago; both rappers were shot to death in separate slayings that have not been solved.

Perhaps coincidentally, rapper Lil' Kim is on trial for perjury and conspiracy in connection with another shooting that occurred outside the same hip-hop station in 2001. Lil' Kim is accused of lying about the incident to protect the alleged shooters.

Black kids are expected to shoot each other, and nobody cares? Well I care, and I think somebody should do something about it.

Meanwhile, *Newsweek* reported this week [March 2005] that the federal government is investigating the entire rap industry for alleged crimes; already, Irv Gotti, head of The Inc. label, was arrested earlier this year on money laundering charges. A federal indictment alleges the label, home to Ja Rule and Ashanti, was part of a murderous criminal enterprise that protected its interstate crack and heroin operation with calculated street assassinations.

Stopping the Glorification of Violence

Sharpton stressed that he was not targeting 50 Cent or The Game in his new crusade, and noted he did not know what role, if any, the two had in the shooting. But he did say there should be a process in which violent acts involving rap acts are punished by denying them publicity on the airwaves.

"The whole body politic of America addressed [singer] Janet Jackson's breast, and it didn't hurt anybody," he said of the infamous Super Bowl flashing. "Here you have actual bloodshed, and people are not even responding at federally regulated radio stations. . . . [B]lack kids are expected to shoot each other, and nobody cares? Well I care, and I think somebody should do something about it."

A request for comment to Universal Music Group—the parent company of 50 Cent's label Interscope—was not immediately returned, nor was a request put into MTV or Sony BMG.

A representative for Hot 97 (WQHT-FM in New York) said the radio station meets Federal Communications Commission standards.

"We in no way condone acts of violence," station spokesman Alex Dudley said. "We hope that the perpetrators of these violent acts are prosecuted to the fullest extent of the law by the proper authorities."

Bryan Leach, a vice president at TVT Records (home to platinum-selling rappers such as Lil Jon and the East Side Boyz and the Ying Yang Twins), said he wasn't sure Sharpton's proposal was the right way to resolve rap-related violence. But he conceded the issue needed to be addressed.

"I think we can be vocal and I think we can show people that it's something that concerns us just like piracy concerns us," he said. "Violence in songs and violence in terms of how it translates in society, in particular the black community, is something that concerns a large part of the record industry."

Leach said he was also concerned that the media was sensationalizing the events of the past week and potentially inflaming the situation.

"A lot of it doesn't seem to be coming from people who really understand the history, really understand the parties involved, really understand a lot of the facts," he said.

Rap Listeners Are Prone to Violence

Pacific Institute for Research and Evaluation

The Pacific Institute for Research and Evaluation (PIRE) is one of the nation's preeminent independent nonprofit public health organizations. It is dedicated to improving health, safety, and well-being through the application of science for the public good.

Young people who listen to rap and hip hop music are more likely to have problems with alcohol, drugs and violence than listeners of other types of music, a new study shows. The link to these problems raises serious questions about the alcohol industry's use of rap and hip hop to market products, the study author said.

A survey of more than 1,000 community college students found that rap music was consistently associated with alcohol use, potential alcohol use disorder, illicit drug use and aggressive behavior. Alcohol and illicit drug use were also associated with listening to techno and reggae. The results were not affected by the respondents' gender or ethnicity.

Young people may be influenced by frequent exposure to music lyrics that make positive references to substance use and violence.

"People should be concerned about rap and hip hop being used to market alcoholic beverages, given the alcohol, drug and aggression problems among listeners," said lead author Meng-Jinn Chen, Ph.D., a research scientist at PIRE Prevention Research Center. "That's particularly true considering the popularity of rap and hip hop among young people."

Rap and hip hop music and artists have been used in commercials and advertisements for malt liquor and other alcohol products, while the urban contemporary music radio format, which features rap and hip hop, is regularly used for alcohol advertising.

A Relationship Between Bad Habits and Rap Music

The study, published today [April 17, 2006] in the May issue of the *Journal of Studies on Alcohol*, surveyed over 1,000 students aged 15 to 25. Students were asked about their music listening habits, alcohol use, illicit drug use and aggressive behaviors—such as getting into fights and attacking or threatening others. Researchers emphasize that the survey results cannot determine whether listening to certain music genres leads to alcohol or illicit drug use or aggressive behavior. Young people with tendencies to use alcohol or illicit drugs or to be aggressive may be drawn to particular music styles.

"While we don't fully understand the relationship between music preferences and behavioral outcomes, our study shows that young people may be influenced by frequent exposure to music lyrics that make positive references to substance use and violence," Meng-Jinn said.

Recent studies of popular music by other researchers reveal that nearly half of rap/hip hop songs mentioned alcohol as compared to around 10 percent or less of other popular music genres. Nearly two-thirds of rap songs mentioned illicit drugs as compared with one-tenth of songs from other genres. Rap and rock music videos depict violence twice as often as other music genres.

The PIRE study, entitled "Music, Substance Use and Aggression," also found that young people who listen to reggae and techno used more alcohol and illicit drugs than listeners of other music, with the exception of rap. Rap topped all other genres in association to alcohol and drug use and aggression.

The study was funded by the National Institute on Alcohol Abuse and Alcoholism (NIAAA). The PIRE Prevention Research Center is sponsored by NIAAA. PIRE, or Pacific Institute for Research and Evaluation, is a national nonprofit public health research institute with centers in seven cities and funded largely by federal grants and contracts.

Stereotypes of Violent Rap Musicians Are Inaccurate

Sarah Benson

Sarah Benson is the lead reporter for the Web site Lawrence
.com, *which covers culture and media for the city of Lawrence,
Kansas.*

Anthony Vital's bullet-riddled body was recently found by
police in a field outside Lawrence, [Kansas].

At first, no details were released. Police didn't announce
the cause of death until three days into the investigation. But
that didn't stop some locals, armed with deep-seated stereotypes, from forming their own conclusions.

Vital—otherwise known as "Clacc" of local rap group Da
BombSquad—had fallen victim to hip-hop.

Or at least that's what some reader posts to the comment
boards at ljworld.com insisted.

An Oct. 17 [2006] post read:

> *"the facts have not been released, but considering he was con-
> sidered a gangster rapper I am guessing he got shot. Sometimes
> it's just too easy to know what happened."*

Another, posted the next day, read:

> *"Another crap-singing (I meant to say rap) wanna-be with as-
> sault charges against him. Tsk-Tsk Ho-Hum what do you ex-
> pect. These people seem to run around in circles of violence.
> They adore it. They sing it. They love it. They live by it, and
> they die by it. Sounds to me like I'm glad he's gone."*

Stereotyping Rap Artists

That comment ignited a week-long online debate that became
less about Clacc and more about the stereotype that black
people + rap music = violent criminals.

Those who knew Clacc have been hit hardest by such re-
marks. Richard Thomas, a.k.a. GQ the Country Bunkin of Da
BombSquad, was a longtime friend of Clacc.

"Unfortunately, my friend was one of those -statistics that
ended up being one of those stereotypes. So it's kind of ugly
from that perspective," GQ says.

"The people that's just like, 'good riddance,' they don't
know Anthony, they ain't never heard his music, they not his
fans. He's just a dead rapper, it's nothing to them."

Nevertheless, those who harbor negative stereotypes about
the so-called "rap lifestyle" believe the facts support their
views. Indeed there has been a string of local incidents that, at
least on the surface, could serve to deepen existing stereotypes.

In just the last year: a 46-year-old man was shot to death
outside of the Granada following a hip-hop concert there;
gunshots have been fired inside Last Call during the club's
popular hip-hop night; in the parking lot outside the same
club, police have seized several weapons including a sawed-off
shotgun and an AK-47 [assault rifle]; and now a Lawrence
rapper is found murdered.

The myth . . . is that all hip-hop music glorifies violence,
promotes gangbanging and drugs and misogynistic sex
and crime and so on and so forth.

As incidents like these become more frequent, area night-
clubs are starting to take measures to preemptively ward off
more violence. Before entering Last Call, for example, patrons
must pass through a metal detector that ensures (according to
the club's answering machine—listen) "the safest nightclub experience anywhere." Other bars in town have implemented
new dress codes that would seem to specifically target hip-hop
crowds. Banned attire includes jerseys, baseball caps turned
sideways, and baggy pants and jackets that cover back pockets.

(The few local clubs that reportedly impose dress codes did not return repeated calls for comment.)

Myth Versus Reality

Jeffrey Mack, a KU [Kansas University] English doctoral student who taught a class on hip-hop culture, calls the dress codes "silly."

"I don't think moderating dress is going to change anything," Mack says. "I think they're focusing on the wrong thing ... this stuff perpetuates the whole myth, negative stereotypes."

The myth, Mack explains, is that all hip-hop music glorifies violence, promotes gangbanging and drugs and misogynistic sex and crime and so on and so forth. He says that people view only a small part of the hip-hop spectrum and judge the entire genre based on a few artists. The rap artists that get the most visibility are also some of the most controversial.

"We overlook people like Mos Def, and we overlook people like Common," Mack says. "All these people that have certain consciousness and social responsibility embedded in their art, they aren't talked about a lot."

High-profile, controversial gangsta rap acts like Public Enemy and NWA [Niggaz with Attitude], Mack says, formed as a sort of "social response mechanism" in the '80s.

"They had a reason behind it," Mack says. "They sort of centralized themselves in relation to that oppression, to say, 'I'm not going to take it anymore, I'm not going to be beaten by the police, I'm not going to be abused by the system. I'm my own man.'"

Now, Mack adds, that gangsta rap movement has evolved into less of a social response mechanism and more into a profitable subgenre of music. 50 Cent, Eminem and Snoop Dogg all rap about violence. But does that mean that even those rap artists are promoting violence or perpetuating it? Are such lyrics at all related to actual murders?

Yes and no, Mack says. But mostly no.

"The way that we look at hip-hop now is the way that we should look at a lot of things in American society. I mean, sex sells. Violence in movies sells. You've got *Saw* one, two and three, you're chopping people's feet off, know what I'm saying?" Mack says. "I think it's interesting that people are singling out one art form and sort of overlooking some of the others."

Profit Is the Bottom Line

GQ of Da BombSquad admits that when it comes to the content of his raps, it's all about the, er, Benjamins [money].

When people go to the club ... they want to hear about smokin' and they want to hear about girls poppin' they butt and the drinks they gonna drink.

"We live in a college town," he says. "If the college students wanted to hear 'peace my brother, let's just love one another,' then that's what we would rap about. 'Cuz we want them to buy our CD. That's what our whole CD gonna be about.

"But when people go to the club and they want to hear about smokin' and they want to hear about girls poppin' they butt and the drinks they gonna drink ... they not gonna buy your CD if you're talkin' about 'get right, my brother.' So as the artist, I got to pick and choose. Am I in the music business or am I a musician?"

GQ, who grew up in South Central L.A. and moved to Kansas at 13, has seen firsthand what most Lawrence hip-hop fans only hear about through white ears.

"By the time I was 18, I had so many friends that I grew up with in L.A. either in jail or went to the penitentiary or done killed somebody or killed, already dead," GQ says. "I'm here in Kansas and it's like 'Dang! It's sad to hear that, but I'm glad my mama sent me out here!'"

Aaron Yates, a.k.a, rapper Tech N9ne, had similar experiences growing up in Kansas City.

"I grew up in Wayne Minor Projects, you know what I'm sizzlin'?" Tech says. "I'm not afraid to say I've sold crack before, but it wasn't for me. I sold it for a family member. I've been through all those gangster things. I grew up in a Blood neighborhood ... I've seen gangsters die, I've seen dope dealers die, I've seen them go to jail. I've got an understanding that that ain't the kind of life that I want to lead."

Both rappers say that in order to be "real," they have to address those life experiences, however bitter, in rhyme.

Tech adds that he doesn't see his sometimes-violent lyrical content as glorifying violence. Instead, he says, he's telling his audience what *not* to do. At the end of some songs (for example, one in which he recounts the night he took 15 hits of ecstacy), there's a disclaimer ("this is my f----- up life").

Who Is Responsible?

The question might well be: Should rappers be held responsible for what they say? In a nation founded on free speech, why is hip-hop targeted as the scapegoat art form that stirs up the most trouble among youth?

In a nation founded on free speech, why is hip-hop targeted as the scapegoat art form that stirs up the most trouble among youth?

Why aren't video games like *Grand Theft Auto*, movies like the *Saw* trilogy, and, as Sean Hunt (a.k.a. Lawrence rapper Approach) adds, country music similarly targeted?

"Listen to Johnny Cash records," he says. "Johnny Cash is killing people in every record he ever made. It's just like, he's an American hero. Your average urban minority is a menace. . . . Music is music. It's entertainment just like any-thing else. Arnold Schwarzenegger kills a million people in his movies, yet he's governor [of California], you know?"

But while he tries to fight rap's bad rap, Approach says that he feels a social responsibility as an artist.

"If you're making music, if you're making anything that puts you in the spotlight, you've gotta be sure you're repre-senting yourself in a responsible manner. If you're presenting the harder aspect of music, the harder aspect of life, you've also got to be arming the kids with 'Hey, this is what I've come from, these are things I've seen, but here's ways to achieve outside of these things," Approach says.

Approach is by no means a gangsta rapper. He admits that he doesn't look like "the big, intimidating black rappers" you'd see on BET or even in Da BombSquad. He also raps to mostly white crowds (Lawrence's population, after all, is just 5 per-cent black). He says he's sure that if anything ever happened at one of his shows—a pistol-whipping, a drug bust, etc.—he'd be automatically classified as "just another rapper having people get shot at his shows."

Sensational Media Representations

Approach partly blames the media for the popular equating of rap with violence.

"You can't say a shooting took place out on Mass Street. It had to be a shooting related to a hip-hop show being played at the Granada that had no fights, no incidents," says Ap-proach, who has worked as the Granada's assistant manager.

He remembers when, early this year, the Granada, and es-pecially hip-hop music, took the blame for a shooting that took place 20 minutes after the club had closed and the con-cert had ended.

Violence like that can leave local clubs scrambling to boost their public image. Hence, dress codes and metal detectors.

But there's not much you can do to stop people who come to public settings specifically to cause trouble.

GQ says that Kansas City hip-hop scenesters come to Lawrence to do just that. He explains that their scene already has "a stamp on it." Insurance companies charge more money there to insure hip-hop shows, which GQ says is forcing the K.C. [Kansas City] scene to spill into Lawrence.

"To get a hip-hop show, they gotta come to Lawrence," GQ says. "It's so expensive to put on a hip-hop show in Kansas City because of violence. . . . They want to tear the club up (in Lawrence) so we don't get to come back and perform in front of our crowd. I think it's a matter of competition."

Effects of Stereotyping

Travis O'Guin, who manages Tech N9ne, also says that insurance rates are getting high enough to make him wonder if there's discrimination at work.

"It's specifically targeted at hip-hop, I mean specifically," O'Guin says. "It's at the point where someone needs to take action and say, 'Hey, what's really going on? What type of discrimination are you really putting on this?'"

"It's at the point where someone needs to take action and say, 'Hey, what's really going on?'"

The problem with the discrimination is that it's not targeted at only the hip-hop groups that attract what O'Guin calls the "hardcore gangster" crowd. It's targeted at all hip-hop, regardless of lyrical content, audience makeup, or the venue's record of violence.

But Tech N9ne, who doesn't have a track record of violence at his shows, admits that some of the discrimination, the negative stereotypes, are "well deserved."

"A lot of us rappers give other rappers a bad name, you know what I'm sizzlin,' because this is from the street. And it is going to bring that element. But I can't imagine in Lawrence, Kansas," he says. "Hip-hop ain't takin' off. We don't have Def Jam Midwest, we don't have Universal Midwest, it's like what are we doin' down here.

"What is rap doin' that'll kill you down here? What has rap done for Clacc that made somebody want to kill him? That's a weird thing to say."

Violent Rap Lyrics Are Not a Significant Contributor to Violent Behavior

Pat Stack

Pat Stack is a regular contributor to the British monthly Socialist Review *and a disability rights activist.*

I remember just after the Columbine massacre [at a Colorado high school in April 1999, in which fifteen died and twenty-three were wounded] hearing some right wing American shock-jock being interviewed as to why the massacre had happened. The music of Marilyn Manson, video nasties, and lack of parental control were all cited. When the interviewer asked whether gun control might not help, the shock-jock dismissed this as so much liberal hooey.

Now it may seem obvious that CDs or indeed videos are not much use as weapons of any kind of destruction, and that a gun is, by any standards, a potentially lethal weapon. But it didn't even occur to this jerk that he sounded absurd. Yet cultural manifestations of some of the nastier aspects of society are far easier to put forward than the realities of life that might have created these nastier aspects.

Blaming Rap Music

The rather glib Blairite [referring to former British prime minister Tony Blair] rallying cry of 'Tough on crime, tough on the causes of crime' becomes even glibber when a [British] government minister reveals that the 'causes of crime' are actually a motley group of rappers. He later added violent PlayStation games. That, though, appears to be what 'culture' (god help us) secretary Kim Howells believes. In the aftermath of

Pat Stack, "Talking Rap," *Socialist Review*, February 2003. www.socialistreview.org.uk. Reproduced by permission.

the Birmingham shootings [in England in January 2003, in which two teenage girls were killed] we need apparently look no further than rap music in general and the 'macho idiot rappers' of So Solid Crew in particular, and video games, to explain 'gun culture', 'black on black crime', and general 'lawlessness' and 'hooliganism'.

This black on black crime stuff fascinates me. I live in an area of London where there have been a number of violent drug-related deaths over the past few months, and the ethnic mix of killers and killed has been great. Nobody in the area is going on about Greek on Italian crime or second generation Irish or English crime.

[So Solid Crew's] music merely reflected "real life issues and what's going on on the streets . . . you can't blame So Solid for all the gun violence out there."

How handy, though, that music and video are there so that we don't need any of that liberal guff about poverty, lack of resources, alienation, or any of those other things that Blair has failed to deal with to explain violent crime. Like the mad rantings of the shock-jock, one is forced to stand back from this and wonder at the inanity of it all.

Indeed how strange that this pillar of the New Labour [political party] intelligentsia needs to have a member of So Solid Crew explain to him that their music merely reflected 'real life issues and what's going on on the streets . . . you can't blame So Solid for all the gun violence out there'. So banal is this truism, that you would hardly think it worth stating. Yet clearly it has passed Howells by. . . .

Oversimplifying the Causes of Violence

It is crucial that the left doesn't fall for his [Howells's] line. True, some rap lyrics are unpleasant, nihilistic, homophobic, and/or misogynist, and some of the artists are far from pleasant people. Yet rap also finds an echo in the realities of modern urban life, and reflects anger and alienation, and to cast haughty judgement on it is little better than my parents telling me that the Rolling Stones were nasty and that you 'couldn't hear the words'.

Ah, it's said, but their violent lyrics are causing all the violence. Now it would be foolish of me to say that there isn't some vulnerable messed up soul out there who, having listened to the lyrics of some song, decided to do something violent. But I have no idea where this gets us. After all, the guy who tried to assassinate Ronnie Regan [U.S. president Ronald Reagan] claimed that his love for [actress] Jodie Foster, after having seen her in the classic 'Taxi Driver', was the cause for his act of violence. Should we conclude that the film should be banned (or, come to think of it, shown daily in all public places)?

An entire terrorist movement in the United States in the late 1960s, the Weathermen, took their name from a line in a Bob Dylan song. When Charles Manson and his crew murdered Sharon Tate and others they scrawled the words 'Piggies' all over the wall. It was a direct lift from a Beatles song. Indeed the Beatles recorded a song which went 'Happiness is a warm gun, bang bang shoot shoot'. No doubt it became an anthem for 'white on white crime' at the time.

I also think I have discovered the origin of Al Qaida. A singer in the 1960s released a song called 'I'm Gonna Get Me A Gun'. It included the lines,

'And all those people who put me
down
You better get ready to run
Cuz I'm gonna get me a gun.'

His name was Cat Stevens. He later changed it to Yusuf Islam on converting to Islam. Now I reckon that in his preradical days when he lived in London [al Qaeda leader] Osama Bin Laden would, on his way to watch [English soccer team]

Arsenal on a Saturday afternoon, be listening to his co-religionist's classic on a Walkman [portable music player], and as a result turned to the gun and violent means to reach his political ends.

Ah, to live in the simple world of Kim Howells—lock up [*Taxi Driver* director] Martin Scorsese, Bob Dylan, the Beatles, Cat Stevens, Eminem and So Solid Crew and you've done away with all the evil in the world. No drug-related crime, no urban terror, no mad assassins, no 11 September [2001, terrorist attacks on America], and all at little or no cost.

Organizations to Contact

The editors have compiled the following list of organizations concerned with the issues debated in this book. The descriptions are derived from materials provided by the organizations. All have publications or information available for interested readers. The list was compiled on the date of publication of the present volume; names, addresses, phone and fax numbers, and e-mail and Internet addresses may change. Be aware that many organizations take several weeks or longer to respond to inquiries, so allow as much time as possible.

AllHipHop
244 Fifth Ave., Ste. 2528, New York, NY   10001
(877) 499-5111
e-mail:grouchygreg@tmail.com
Web site: http://allhiphop.com/default.aspx

AllHipHop was founded in 1998 to become a resource for hip-hop artists and fans on the Internet, featuring daily news, interviews, reviews, multimedia, and community connections. In addition to providing a Web site, AllHipHop.com, All-HipHop has been delivering daily news alerts to music industry tastemakers and hip-hop enthusiasts using two-way pagers, cell phones, and e-mail addresses.

Concerned Women of America (CWA)
1015 Fifteenth St., Ste. 1100, Washington, DC   20005
(202) 488-7000 • fax: (202) 448-0806
e-mail: mail@cwfa.org
Web site: www.cwfa.org

CWA seeks to protect the interests of American families, promote biblical values, and provide a voice for women throughout the United States who believe in Judeo-Christian values. CWA believes that sexually explicit popular culture contributes to the decline of families and interferes with raising healthy children. CWA publishes the bimonthly *Family Voice* and numerous press releases and reports, including "Sexually Explicit Media and Children" and "Music's Deadly Influence."

Culture Shock
2110 Hancock St., Ste. 200, San Diego, CA   92110
(619) 299-2110
Web site: www.cultureshockdance.org

Culture Shock is a nonprofit hip-hop dance troupe dedicated to offering children and youth in diverse communities an alternative to street life by providing a rewarding activity and instilling confidence. Founded in 1993, Culture Shock has grown from its home location of San Diego, California, to cities across the United States, Canada, and the United Kingdom.

The Heritage Foundation
214 Massachusetts Ave. NE, Washington, DC   20002-4999
(800) 544-4843
e-mail: info@heritage.org
Web site: www.heritage.org

The Heritage Foundation is a conservative public policy organization dedicated to individual liberty, free-market principles, and limited government. It advises parents to restrict the music and movies that children and youth consume. Its resident scholars publish position papers on a wide range of issues, including "A Culture Awash in Porn" and "The Culture War: A Five-Point Plan for Parents."

Hip-Hop Association (H2A)
PO Box 1181, New York, NY   10035
(718) 682-2744 • fax: (866) 540-0384
e-mail: info@hiphopassociation.org
Web site: www.hiphopassociation.org

Founded in 2002, H2A works to facilitate critical thinking and foster constructive social change and unity to instill tolerance, civic participation, social reform, and economic sustainability, while advancing hip-hop culture through innovative programming. H2A organizes an international film festival and publishes the monthly *Defuse News*, a news and information report that includes commentary, announcements, and resources such as grants, fellowships, and job opportunities.

Hip-Hop Theater Festival (HHTF)
57 Thames St., Ste. 4B, Brooklyn, NY   11237
(718) 497-4282 • fax: (718) 497-4240
e-mail: clyde@hiphoptheaterfest.org
Web site: www.hiphoptheaterfest.org

The mission of HHTF is to promote hip-hop theater as a recognized genre by commissioning and developing new work and helping artists build coalitions, collaborations, and networks with other artists and institutions around the United States and the world. The organization presents live events created by artists who combine a variety of theatrical forms, including theater, dance, spoken word, and live music sampling. HHTF also strives to bring new, younger audiences to the theater in large numbers, in an effort to ensure the future of live performance.

Morality in Media (MIM)
475 Riverside Dr., Ste. 239, New York, NY   10115
(212) 870-3222 • fax: (212) 870-2765
e-mail: mim@moralityinmedia.org
Web site: www.moralityinmedia.org

MIM is an interfaith organization that fights pornography and opposes indecency in the mainstream media. It maintains the National Obscenity Law Center, a clearinghouse of legal materials on obscenity law. MIM publishes the bimonthly publications *Morality in Media* and *Obscenity Law Bulletin* and several papers, including "Hip-Hop Misogyny: A Destructive Force," "Altered Perceptions—Media and Youth," and "Mass Murder and Popular Culture."

National Congress of Black Women (NCBW)
1224 W. St. SE, Ste. 200, Washington, DC   20020
(202) 678-6788
e-mail: info@nationalcongressbw.org
Web site: www.nationalcongressbw.org

The NCBW supports the advancement of African American women in politics and government. The congress also engages in research on critical issues that affect the quality of life of African American women and youth. Through its Commission on Entertainment, the NCBW campaigns against the glorification of violence, misogyny, pornography, and drugs in popular entertainment. It publishes project reports on its Web site, including "Crusading Against Gangsta/Porno Rap."

Bibliography

Books

Michael Eric Dyson — *Know What I Mean? Reflections on Hip-Hop*. New York: Basic Civitas, 2007.

Eileen M. Hayes and Linda F. Williams, eds. — *Black Women and Music: More than the Blues*. Urbana: University of Illinois Press, 2007.

Mickey Hess — *Is Hip Hop Dead? The Past, Present, and Future of America's Most Wanted Music*. Westport, CT: Praeger, 2007.

Kenji Jasper and Ytasha L. Womack, eds. — *Beats, Rhymes, & Life: What We Love and Hate About Hip-Hop*. New York: Harlem Moon, 2007.

Johan Kugelberg — *Born in the Bronx: A Visual Record of the Early Days of Hip-Hop*. New York: Rizzoli, 2007.

Cameron Lazerine — *Rap-Up: The Ultimate Guide to Hip-Hop and R & B*. New York: Grand Central, 2007.

Tayannah Lee McQuillar — *When Rap Music Had a Conscience: The Artists, Organizations, and Historic Events that Inspires and Influenced the "Golden Age" of Hip-Hop from 1987 to 1996*. New York: Thunder's Mouth, 2007.

Halifu Osumare	*The Africanist Aesthetic in Global Hip-Hop: Power Moves.* New York: Palgrave Macmillan, 2007.
Roni Sarig	*Third Coast: Outkast, Timbaland, and How Hip-Hop Became a Southern Thing.* New York: Da Capo, 2007.
Ida Walker	*Hip-hop Around the World.* Philadelphia: Mason Crest, 2008.
Rosa Waters	*Hip-Hop: A Short History.* Bromall, PA: Mason Crest, 2007.

Periodicals

Joy T. Bennett	"What Do We Tell Our Children?" *Ebony*, July 2007.
Mariel Concepcion	"David Banner: Rapper/Producer David Banner Has Become One of the Most Vocal Defenders of Hip Hop Lyrics," *Billboard*, October 6, 2007.
Antonio D'Ambrosio	"Chuck D.," *Progressive*, August 2005.
Imani A. Dawson	"Good Rap, Bad Rap: Hip-hop Conference Empowers Young Black Women to Change the Game," *Ms*, Summer 2005.
Michael Eric Dyson	"Is Hop-Hop Dead?" *Ebony*, June 2007.

Dimitri Ehrlich "Common: Why Hip-hop's Square Peg Refuses to Live Up to His Name," *Interview*, October 2007.

Dorinda Elliott "You Got to Have Guts: Sure, There's Racism. This Hop-hop Mogul Says That's No Excuse," *Time*, November 14, 2005.

Chloe A. Hilliard "Girls to Men," *Village Voice*, April 11, 2007.

Nadira A. Hira "America's Hippest CEO: Rapper and Entrepreneur Jay-Z (a.k.a. Shawn Carter) Brings His Own Style to the Corner Office at Def Jam," *Fortune*, October 17, 2005.

Michael Kimmelman "In Marseille, Rap Helps Keep the Peace," *New York Times*, December 12, 2007.

Gail Mitchell "6 Questions with Ludacris," *Billboard*, September 30, 2006.

Joan Morgan "They Call Me Ms. Hill," *Essence*, February 2006.

Carol M. Motley and Geraldine Henderson "The Global Hip-hop Diaspora: Understanding the Culture," *Journal of Business Research*, March 2008.

Miguel Munoz-Laboy, Hannah Weinstein, and Richard Parker "The Hip-Hop Club Scene: Gender, Grinding and Sex," *Culture*, November/December 2007.

Jessica Pallay — "Making Waves: An Interview with Curtis '50 Cent' Jackson," *Daily News Record*, February 26, 2007.

Tara Parker-Pope — "For Clues on Teenage Sex, Experts Look to Hip-Hop," *New York Times*, November 6, 2007.

Jody Rosen — "A Rolling Shout-Out to Hip-Hop History," *New York Times*, February 12, 2006.

Kelefa Sanneh — "Don't Blame Hip-Hop," *New York Times*, April 25, 2007.

Vivienne Tam — "Marketing the Realities of Urban Life," *Time*, May 8, 2006.

DeWayne Wickham — "Black Fashion Statements Send the Wrong Message," *USA Today*, October 9, 2007.

Index